The Happening

NICKEL MINES SCHOOL TRAGEDY

Vision Publishers
PO Box 190
Harrisonburg, VA 22803

www.vision-publishers.com
ph. - 877.488.0901 • fax - 540.437.1969
email - cs@vision-publishers.com
We Welcome Your Response!

ISBN: 978-1-885270-70-2

Cover Design: Gloria Miller

First Printing: August 2007

Second Printing: October 2007

Third Printing: October 2007

Fourth Printing: October 2007

Printed in the USA

Back cover photo: Randy Karr

For more information about Christian Aid Ministries, see pages 172-173.

To order additional copies of *The Happening*, please contact:

TGS International
PO Box 355
Berlin, Ohio 44610 USA
Phone: 330·893·2428
Fax: 330·893·2305
Email: tgsbooks@camoh.org

The
Happening

Nickel Mines School Tragedy

Harvey Yoder

Table of Contents

Foreword

Forgiveness

The motive behind publishing *The Happening* was not to retell the tragic details of October 2, 2006, but to preserve in print the inspiring response of forgiveness by the victims' families. We felt this active portrayal of "turning the other cheek" could challenge us and other people around the world to forgive others as Christ forgave us.

We live in a wonderful world God created and called good. However, more and more we read about terrible things happening in faraway places, in our own country, and, increasingly, in our backyards. We read of broken homes, robberies, murders, and much more. All this evil comes from the fallen sin nature of man, and it causes much sadness, suffering, bitterness, and unforgiveness.

We often read of victims or their families cursing those who have wronged them. How startlingly refreshing to see the reaction of the grieving fathers and mothers of the innocent children who were so brutally killed and wounded at Nickel Mines. Instead of hate and revenge, they offered forgiveness.

As the news spread around the world, many considered these Amish families almost supernatural in their ability to forgive. But as believers and followers of Jesus Christ, what other options do we have? Christ's teachings are clear: Love your enemies, bless those who curse you, do good to those who hate you, and pray for those who despitefully use you. In the Lord's Prayer, He taught us to forgive those who wrong us.

Man's natural inclination when wronged is to revenge. Even dedicated Christians struggle with conflicting emotions and sometimes have to forgive over and over. But we all have a choice. Love and forgiveness can hardly be separated. Neither can hate and revenge. God gave each of us a will which only we can exercise. We have to choose between love and hate, forgiveness and revenge. Our feelings are not sufficient for the task. We must make a conscious choice, and our feelings will follow. When we examine these decisions in the light of Christ's New Testament teachings, the right choice becomes obvious.

Comments and condolences flooded in from around the world regarding this unfortunate happening. One of the most unexpected messages came from the suffering Christians of North Korea. They wrote:

"At this difficult moment for Amish, we are with you in our prayers. We beg God to give to your peace-loving families, whose children have died such a cruel and senseless death, the strength to overcome grief and anguish. Our hearts are with you in your anguish."

Undoubtedly the Amish families who endured this terrible loss would say, "We are unprofitable servants: we have done that which was our duty to do" (Luke 17:10).

Forgiveness. When I forgive, I set a prisoner free, and that prisoner is myself.

For if ye forgive men their trespasses, your heavenly Father will also forgive you. Matthew 6:14

David N. Troyer
General Director
Christian Aid Ministries

Prologue

Everyone agrees that the Monday morning of October 2, 2006, was exceptionally bright and sunny in Pennsylvania. The trees were still green, hardly showing a hint of the autumn color that would dot the countryside in just a few weeks. The warm sun rising over the horizon shone on the gently rolling farms of southeastern Lancaster County.

The Nickel Mines community, named for the ore mined there during the second half of the nineteenth century, is mostly a farming community where the Amish have lived for generations, raising their families and tilling the fertile soil with their workhorses, living alongside the many non-Amish people who also populate the area. It is a community where people are used to waving at their acquaintances as they pass on the roads, whether they are driving cars and trucks or horses and buggies. The people of Nickel Mines plow their fields, tend their stores, and work in their shops just like people in thousands of other rural communities all over America.

On that sunny morning, many people were already at work in woodworking shops, small manufacturing businesses, or at home on their dairy farms. Buses had already picked up children to take them to the public schools, and the Amish children had already walked, for the most part, to their small one-room schools, usually almost within sight of their homes.

There are over 175 of these Amish schools in Lancaster County alone, most of them taught by young single women who teach first grade through eighth grade, the last year of formal education. For this privilege of teaching their own children the Amish have struggled long and hard—and won.

The tragedy and heartbreak that entered one of these Amish schools on that Monday morning shocked the nation and the world.

A lone gunman—who in notes to his wife and in brief statements to his hostages blamed the death of his firstborn infant and other unverified incidents—brought the community together in a way he could never have imagined in his wildest, most deranged moments.

The quick response of the officers, the massive support

system of surrounding police and fire departments, and the immediate deployment of ambulances and hospital helicopters astounded the community.

Ten victims were the center of the catastrophe as police officers carried the wounded and dying out of the schoolhouse. The gunman was already dead, but as the carnage was being dealt with, feelings ran high.

In the days that followed, people all over the world were glued to the news and read articles in newspapers and magazines. Professionals tried to piece together what had happened, and the police and local fire personnel shifted from dealing with the victims to handling the swarms of people descending on the community. While the police held the curious at bay, secured the roads, and restricted traffic to local residents, the community planned four funerals for the five young girls who had died. Officers worked long and hard to give the families a measure of privacy to conduct their funerals, but in spite of that many felt their grief was made public by the media.

The lives of the survivors went on. Day by day, bits and pieces of information trickled into and out of the community. Still, it just didn't make sense. Why had the gunman done this? Many of those involved and those who heard about the tragedy were angry and frustrated.

But something began to crystallize through the stories that continued to spread all over the world.

Forgiveness.

The evening after the shootings, an Amishman visited the grandfather of the gunman's widow and offered his condolences. But more than that, he gave the gift of forgiveness.

This is what continued to rivet the attention of the world, even after the initial shock of the massacre wore off. Stories leaked out, telling of Amish families attending the gunman's funeral, and of Amish people contacting the widow to assure her that they held no malice toward her in their hearts.

Follow the story of Rebecca Sue, who was in the Nickel Mines School. Although her name is fictitious, the facts surrounding her story are real. The events and conversations of that Monday and the days that followed have been reconstructed as accurately as possible, down to the description of the classroom and the very songs they sang in school that morning. In consideration of the Amish community's desire for anonymity, and to protect the privacy of the teacher, students, and parents, other names have also been changed. In respect for their desire for privacy, the experiences attributed to Rebecca Sue happened to more than just one of the girls. Likewise, Rebecca Sue's family is a combination of several families in the community. Nevertheless, the happenings and the emotions are true.

Lest you criticize the attempt to mask the true identity of the people in the story, consider for a moment the enormous amount of pressure already inflicted upon the victims. Not only have many lost a daughter, a sister, a classmate, or a friend, but the world has been looking over their shoulders and into their private lives during their grief. That is never easy, especially for the Amish, who, for the most part, shun the public spotlight.

Therefore, for the sake of those directly involved, it is good for the rest of us to hold back our curiosity in order to allow the families their privacy and the chance to get their lives back, as someone put it, to a "new normal."

1

My Home

Looking back, I still marvel at the absolute beauty of that Monday morning in October. I remember standing outside on our back porch, pegging clothes onto the pulley wash line, the early morning sunshine streaming through the maple trees in our yard and bathing everything with gold.

I heard the sparrows chattering out in the barnyard, squabbling about some important matter like they always do. Somewhere in a high branch a robin sang cheerily, then stopped to scold when a barn cat crept around the corner of the shed.

"Rebecca Sue! Are you finished?" Mom called through the open window.

I bent hastily and grabbed another towel. "Almost," I replied.

I could hear the clattering of plates as my ten-year-old sister, Sadie Mae, set the table for breakfast, sprinting around the kitchen table on her quick bare feet.

I gave the clothesline a tug, moving the clothes farther up the incline toward the top of the distant pole Dad had erected to anchor the pulley. Looking out across the fields, I could see someone hanging out wash at the John Beiler place. Maybe it was Hannah, my good friend and schoolmate. I waved my arm to see if anyone was looking my way, but I couldn't see well enough to know who was there. Their clothesline was filling up fast, as was mine. I could picture my friend lifting clean clothes from her wash basket and hanging them up to dry. I would ask her in school if she had seen me.

"Rebecca Sue! Where are you?" Mom's voice—and the hint of impatience in it—jerked me back from my daydreams.

I jumped guiltily. "I'm almost done," I answered.

I know it's sometimes hard on Mom that I get distracted so easily. Mom is so quick and efficient in everything she does. She gets the work done in a hurry. I am slow by nature, and I have to confess that I have a tendency to daydream. I forced my attention back to the laundry, wishing I could be more like Sadie Mae, who, like Mom, could do a lot in a little time.

"Rebecca Sue! Where are you?"

"Elam!" I jumped and whirled around to face my brother. "You scared me!" Elam is two years older than I, and a wonderful tease.

With a nimble leap, he landed on the back porch beside me. Grabbing the last towel from the wash basket, he snapped it toward me. I jumped back, trying to escape the damp towel. I ran around the picnic table to evade my teasing brother.

A giggle from the doorway distracted me. "Rosebud! Are you up already?" I ran toward my three-year-old sister, who was laughing at our antics. But Sadie Mae, dashing out the side door, grabbed her first and ran off the porch, carrying our squealing sister with her, the two laughing with glee.

I darted after them, my bare toes digging into the grass. Suddenly I felt the snap of a towel on my back.

"Elam! Stop that!" I yelled, turning to face his laughter.

Desperate to be in on the fun, Sadie Mae attacked Elam from the back, shoving him and sending him sprawling on the grass.

Rosie had been hastily set down. Now, seeing her big brother lying on the lawn in front of her, she ran over to him and sat on his stomach. Sadie Mae was throwing handfuls of grass onto Elam while dodging his flailing arms. Roxie, our Jack Russell puppy, joined right in, barking shrilly and bouncing up and down on her short legs.

"Children!" Mom called from the window, "I see Dad and Benuel coming in from the barn. Hurry! Get ready for breakfast!"

Soon all seven of us were gathered around the breakfast table eating our bacon and eggs. It seemed like just another normal day. I have read that sometimes people sense when something terrible is about to happen. Later they look back and realize there were signs warning them of a disaster. But for me, there was nothing. I guess I'm still too young to recognize signs like that.

The picture of that morning is carved into my mind—our family gathered around the table in the big kitchen, talking about everyday things, surrounded by the farmhouse—our home. Framed around that was our farm, including the addition where Mommi and Dawdi, Dad's parents, lived. Out beyond the frame of this picture was the community in which we lived. Beyond that, the world stretched out into unknown and seemingly endless places.

I wonder how long this picture will remain etched in my mind—the picture of when life was normal and everything was just as it should be.

"Is everyone finished eating?" Dad asked as he folded his arms and looked around the table. "Then quiet." Silence fell as we bowed our heads and closed our eyes for the prayer that followed every meal.

I loved the silent times of prayer before and after our meals. It made a safe, special place to be alone with my thoughts. I had a prayer that I repeated in my head, but there were times I forgot the prayer of thanks and other thoughts crept in and took root in my mind.

I don't remember what I thought about that morning. Did I thank God for the food like I should have? Did I ask God to be with me and help me to be good that day? I wish I could remember.

I heard Dad's chair creak, and the buzz of our family rising from their places indicated that breakfast was over.

"Rebecca, get the lunches ready." Mom spoke even as she was getting up from her chair. "Sadie Mae, you clear the table."

"Where is my Rosebud?" Dad pretended he didn't see my little sister. "Is she hiding?"

Rosie giggled and slid off her chair. She slipped under the table and came out the other side.

"What is this?" Benuel laughed. "A little girl under the table?"

Rosie loved this ritual.

"Rebecca Sue . . ." Mom warned as she saw me standing there, watching them play with Rosie.

"Yes, Mom," I answered, and hurried to get the lunch buckets.

The Happening

There was always a flurry of activity on school mornings. We heard a honk outside, and Benuel got up quickly, grabbed the lunch Mom had prepared earlier, and with a hasty "goodbye" rushed out the door to join the rest of the carpentry crew he worked with.

"Do you think Big Jim is telling a story already?" Elam wondered, standing up to look out the window. Big Jim was the jolly driver who took the carpenters to and from their work. "Do you think he will help put the roof on today?"

We all laughed at the idea of Big Jim standing on top of a house, his large frame silhouetted against the bright sky.

"No, I think he will tell stories," Sadie Mae grinned. We all enjoyed the stories that Benuel retold for our benefit in the evenings.

"There goes Corner Sam's rig," Elam said, looking toward the crossroads where White Oak and Mine roads intersected. "I guess someone is taking Teacher Leah to school this morning." I could faintly hear the brisk clip-clop of the horse's shod feet on the blacktop road.

Our teacher's dad was called Corner Sam by all the Amish, and a number of the community people as well. His farm was right on a corner and it helped everyone to know which of the many Sams we were talking about.

"Where is Sadie Mae?" Mom wondered aloud.

Just then we heard Roxie's excited yapping out in the yard. My younger sister's joyous laughter could be traced from window to window as she dashed around the yard after her puppy.

"Ach, what would she do without Roxie?" Dad asked in his deep, slow voice, looking at me with a smile.

"She has found a match for her tireless energy," Elam laughed. He got up and walked outside. I joined him.

Even now, just thinking about it brings a sharp jab to my heart as I remember that picture—Sadie Mae's feet skimming over the green grass, her arms pumping up and down and her black apron plastered against her blue dress. She was a picture of innocence and childhood joy as Roxie ran beside her, leaping up and trying to grab the hem of her skirt. I don't know how it is possible to have such sharp pictures branded into my head, but that is a scene I don't think I will ever forget.

"Girls! Time for school!" Mom reminded us.

Dad and Elam were already out in the shop, where they assembled precut pieces of wood to make lawn furniture. Besides doing the regular farm work on the dairy, they filled their daytime hours with their furniture job.

I know I'm spending a long time telling about my family

and where we live, but I can't get enough of filling my mind with the happy memories of the days when life was so . . . how shall I say it? So . . . well . . . normal. Before the painful events at school that day. Before the happening.

I remember Sadie Mae and me taking our backpacks and starting down the road. We passed Ralph and Teresa Dabney's house. Teresa was outside on her patio drinking her coffee.

"Good morning, girls!" she called out cheerily, waving to us.

"Good morning!" we replied. Then Sadie Mae added, "I'll try to be over this afternoon to help you with your flower beds."

"Do come!" Teresa encouraged her. "It will be a wonderful day to work outside."

The Dabneys had moved to Lancaster County from Philadelphia and had built a new house on some land right beside our farm. They were childless, and as we had become acquainted with them, they had become a part of our lives, and, I think, we of theirs. Even though they were English, as we call the non-Amish, we became quite fond of them. As they grew older, we children often helped them with chores around the yard and in the house.

"I just love their flowers," Sadie Mae commented, skipping

ahead of me on the road. "When I get big, I want to have flowers all around my house."

"We have flowers," I reminded her.

"But the Dabneys have different kinds of flowers!" Sadie Mae told me excitedly. "Mrs. Dabney tells me the names of them and helps me learn all about their growing habits." Suddenly she pointed down the road, grabbing my hand and pulling me along. "Look, there are the Beiler girls!"

I keenly remember the tug of her eager hand in mine, pulling me after her. That's the way it was with us. Even though I was the oldest, my younger sister was always in the lead, darting everywhere, making friends with her quick laugh and brightening our days with her cheerful spirit.

"Were you hanging out wash at your house this morning?" I asked my best friend Hannah, who was also thirteen and in my grade.

"Nope. Mom hung it out this morning. It was my turn to do the washing, so as soon as I finished, I was reading a book in my room."

Hannah loved to read. She was also good at word games and got good grades in her school lessons. Many times she had helped me with my lessons.

I knew I was fortunate to have a friend like her. Always

neat in her appearance, Hannah's hair bun stayed neatly combed and tidily intact no matter how hard she ran and played at school. Not like my hair, which had a tendency to come loose whenever we played some intense game of softball or prisoner's base. Once I was so embarrassed when, in the middle of a flying dash to free someone, I felt my hair tumble down my back, my hairpins flying into the grass. But Hannah had come to my rescue. She had picked up the pins and, ignoring the teasing laughter from the boys, run into the schoolhouse with me to help pin up my hair again.

We shared secrets, wrote notes to each other, and did fun things girls love to do together. There were Sunday afternoons when we walked arm in arm through the woods that joined our farms, talking about our dreams and hopes for the future. We were in the same church district, so we saw each other every other Sunday wherever services were held, as well as daily during the school term.

She, too, had a younger sister. Catherine was three years younger than Hannah, and the two sisters were great friends, just like Sadie Mae and me. I liked being with them, and whenever it was their family's turn to host church services at their house, I tried to make sure I could go help them get ready for that Sunday. They, in turn, sometimes helped us when it was our turn. Of course, that only happened about once a year, since our church district has many families and we all take turns hosting services. Usually we have them in our houses, but sometimes we clean out the woodshops or sheds and have services there.

But that was all before the happening, when my world felt safe and secure and my days were long and full. Each season brought its changes, and the warm days of summer slipped into the delightfully cool days of fall. Like the preachers said in church, *"Frosht und hitz, summa und vinda."* (Frost and heat, summer and winter.) For some reason, that phrase read from our German Bible seems to sum up my childhood days. More than just the changing of the seasons, it was the regularity of the days, each predictable and manageable, that wrapped me in the arms of a safe and happy world. I look back at the girl I was then and am amazed that I am the same girl. In many ways, I suppose I'm not.

2

Our School

On that Monday, as on every school morning, our scholars were walking to school from all directions. Our school was no different than the other Amish schools scattered throughout Lancaster County. We went to our one-room schoolhouses, just as our parents had done, and even some of our grandparents.

My dad told me about the beginnings of our schools. Things were not always as smooth as they are now.

At least forty years ago, Pennsylvania's one-room schoolhouses were consolidated into large public schools. The Amish were concerned about what would happen to their children if they were bused away and placed in large schools.

"Enough people were concerned that we started our own schools," Dad told us. "At first the school officials did not want to let us run our schools the way we believed was right. Fathers were even put in jail because they refused to send their children to the public school."

I guess once the school officials saw that this was something the Amish firmly stood for, they finally gave in. They allowed our people to form our own school boards, hire teachers from our own circles, and decide what books to use in our schools. Today we still benefit from those decisions.

There are at least two other schools in the Nickel Mines area, but ours is—or was—the closest to the Nickel Mines crossroads. Really, Nickel Mines is only a cluster of houses, about eight or so, that line Mine Road, plus the Nickel Mine Auction House, where every other Thursday evening there is an auction where antiques and household items are sold. I have gone there several times with Benuel and Elam. Benuel is sometimes pressed into duty as a runner, taking the sold items from the front to the buyers. Several of the Amish ladies run a food counter where we can buy homemade sandwiches and fresh doughnuts. It's a noisy, happy place where the community people gather to try to snap up bargains. The antique dealers are always there too, buying for their shops in the nearby cities or towns.

The auction house is just an ordinary one-story building, painted an ordinary brown. I think it was at one time a general store, but I'm not sure. The main interest to us children is the soft drink machine beside the front door, where I'm occasionally allowed to get a root beer for a treat. I like the fizzy sting of the soda as it slides down my throat on a warm afternoon.

As we passed the auction house on this Monday morning, I could see some of the other scholars hurrying across the fields from other directions. Our school was just down the road from the crossroads.

"Good morning, girls!" Teacher Leah greeted us as Hannah and I entered the schoolhouse.

I have a wonderful memory of that morning. It was all so normal—so everyday.

Our teacher is a smiley kind of person. She doesn't talk a lot, but is one of the friendliest and most cheerful people I know. Though not much taller than Hannah, she stands straight and tall in the eyes of us scholars. That morning she sat at her desk at the front of the room, and when she looked up at us, her eyes twinkled. She gave a soft chuckle and read from a piece of paper she held in her hands.

"Good morning to you, Teacher dear,

This is a day that brings good cheer

Because we're in school once again,

With our teacher and our friends."

Teacher Leah looked at us with that special sparkle in her eyes. "Now who do you suppose gave me such a nice note of encouragement?"

Hannah nudged me with her elbow. I covered my mouth with my hand to hide a giggle.

"It's such an encouragement for a teacher to find a note like this on a bright Monday morning," Teacher Leah continued, as though talking to herself. "Some students really know how to cheer up the day!"

I knew Hannah had slipped the note under the teacher's plan book the Friday before. We had started writing notes to Teacher Leah soon after school had begun the first of September, just last month. Sometimes I would write a note and sometimes Hannah would. Teacher Leah seemed to know that we eighth-grade girls were responsible, but we tried to disguise our handwriting so she wouldn't know which one of us wrote which note. I suspected she knew, though, because our teacher is pretty smart.

This was the third year Teacher Leah was teaching in our school. She had been only seventeen the year she started, but it had not taken long for us to realize we were in the hands of a good teacher. Although she was friendly and fun loving, she kept order in our school. I remember well the day one of the boys mocked a handicapped boy he had seen at a horse auction. Teacher Leah rebuked him sternly, then talked to us seriously about how we should respond lovingly to those who are mentally handicapped.

"She's just like her father," Mom told me when I related the incident to her after school. "Corner Sam is well known for his kindness and friendliness to everyone."

As you can tell, I like my teacher very much. Her familiar voice is hardly ever raised. She teaches the classes with a pleasant tone and moves about the schoolroom explaining difficult problems to us. I'm glad she is teaching this term, for I wanted her to keep on at least until I finished eighth grade, my last year of school.

Just recently, during our lunch period, one of the little boys declared, "Teacher Leah, I hope you teach until I'm out of school."

One of the older boys laughed and said, "What if she finds a boyfriend and gets married?"

The other boys and some of the girls giggled, but I admired the way Teacher Leah just smiled and talked about something else. That's the way she is.

The Happening

The warning bell rang five minutes before school time, just like always. Then, a little later, the bell drew everyone inside and our school day began.

In the back of the room, the double doors looking out toward the road were open, letting any stray breezes cool us. The windows, too, as well as the side door, were standing open. It was going to be a warm day.

I wish I could remember what chapter Teacher Leah read from that morning. She always opened our school day by reading from the Bible. I do remember singing the song that little Martha, a first-grader, chose. Standing beside my desk, I lifted my voice along with the other twenty-five students, singing,

My heavenly home is bright and fair,
I feel like traveling on.
No pain nor death can enter there,
I feel like traveling on.

I don't remember thinking much about the words that morning. I'd always liked that song, because it somehow echoed something inside of me—something that made me want to answer a beckoning call.

Yes, I feel like traveling on!
I feel like traveling on!

My heavenly home is bright and fair,

I feel like traveling on!

Heaven. I knew that was what we were singing about, but like I said, I did not pay much attention to the words. Not until later did Martha's choice of a song grip me with deep meaning.

The next one we sang was in German.

Bedenke Mensch das Ende,   (Think O man about the end,)

Bedenke deinen Todt.   (Think about your death)

Der Todt kommt oft behende;   (Death often comes quickly;)

Der heute frisch und rot,   (Today you may be healthy and ruddy,)

Kann morgen und geschwinder   (But tomorrow or sooner)

Hinveg gestorben sein.   (You may have passed away.)

Drum bilde dir, o Sünder!   (Keep this in mind, O sinner!)

Ein täglich Sterben ein.   (Be ready to die each day.)

As with the song before, I hardly thought of the words as we sang. All of my childhood, these songs had been woven into my life until they had become a part of me.

I glanced around our cheery schoolroom. Teacher Leah had put up our artwork on the walls between the windows on each side of the room. In the front of the classroom, behind the teacher's desk, stood three blackboards ready for classes. Beside one blackboard, Teacher Leah had made an attractive chart labeled "Visitors Brighten Our Days," followed by spaces where guests signed their names. A vase holding a bouquet of asters stood on one corner of the teacher's desk, a present from one of the little girls.

At first recess we ran outside to play our favorite game, softball. It felt good to be outside after a morning of doing arithmetic.

"Rebecca Sue!" Ammon, one of the big boys, panted when a good hit took him all the way to third base, where I was fielding. "Isn't that your milkman's truck parked up beside the auction house?"

I looked up the hill toward the crossroads. I could see the side of the cab plainly and recognized the long, shiny rig.

"Yes, that's Mr. Roberts' truck."

"I wonder why he's parked there," Ammon said.

"I have no idea," I replied. "Last night I was out in the milk house fetching milk when he stopped by to pick up the milk. He had trouble connecting the hose to our tank and asked me to hold the flashlight for him. When he first said something to me, I was startled, because he hardly ever speaks to us. I guess he only talks when he wants something."

Then Hannah hit a grounder and Ammon dashed for home.

The memory of how the milkman had talked to me that

night seemed insignificant at the time, but later it was one of those things I couldn't forget.

"Teacher Leah!" one of the younger boys shouted when recess was almost over. "Your mom and sister are coming!"

I looked up the road, and, sure enough, I could see a horse pulling an open buggy down the road toward the schoolhouse. It looked like Corner Sam's rig.

The horse slowed from his trot as Teacher Leah's mom, Mary, guided him into the school driveway.

"Yes," Teacher Leah told us. "They had planned to visit last Thursday, but then something came up, so here they are."

Hannah and I went over to meet them. Teacher Leah's sister, Malinda, was only a year older than I and was one of our friends.

Two other women climbed down from the buggy. I recognized Teacher Leah's brothers' wives, Lizzie and Sylvia. Lizzie had brought her two small children, Susie, two years old, and baby Mose, five months old. Sylvia was still a newlywed. She and Jonathan had not been married quite a year yet.

We were used to visitors. Our mothers often visited school, sometimes bringing relatives from other districts. At times some of the local tour guides would arrange with the school board to bring some English visitors to see our school in session. I guess there are lots of curious people who want to see how Amish schools operate.

When the bell rang at 10:15, we all went inside. Teacher Leah put out chairs for the visitors in the back of the room beside the double doors.

My desk was on the right side as you come in, beside Hannah's. The older boys were beside us in the last row, and the youngest ones were up front, with the other grades in between.

As we returned to our studies, the usual quiet was broken only by little Mose, cooing in Malinda's arms. Susie sat on her mother's lap, looking at a book Teacher Leah had given her.

"Time for second-grade reading," Teacher Leah said pleasantly, and the second graders got up from their desks and stood in a semicircle facing our teacher.

Once again, I look back at that morning and marvel at how perfectly normal everything was. I was wearing my new blue dress, and at recess I had fallen and gotten a grass stain on the side. Even though I had tried to clean it off, a green smear still showed where I had fallen.

I also remember glancing down at the new tile floor.

Over the summer vacation our school board had arranged to have tiles installed to make it easier to keep our floors clean. The schoolhouse had been built sometime in the 1980s, so it was still in good repair. Like many other Amish schools, ours was a pale, off-white stucco building. It stood between three maple trees at the edge of Jacob Stoltzfus's farm. The meadows on two sides of the school grounds were pastures for the workhorses. A cornfield, already harvested, was on another side. Two outhouses, one for the boys and one for the girls, stood beside the schoolhouse.

The breeze coming in through the open doors felt good on my flushed cheeks. I glanced back at the visitors and smiled at little Susie, who was looking right at me. She smiled back shyly, and I thought about how little children are like gifts sent from heaven to make our world a brighter place to live.

We couldn't have been working for more than ten minutes when I heard the engine of an approaching vehicle coming down from the crossroads. Instead of speeding up, like most vehicles do as they leave Nickel Mines, this one slowed down. I didn't pay much attention to it, yet now I think back and know that it did make me wonder who was coming. I distinctly heard the crunch of tires on the gravel driveway, and, looking out, I saw a pickup truck backing toward the open double doors.

The Happening

Even now, over six months later, something deep inside of me wants to block out the next hour. The next hours. The next days. The next weeks.

3

The Happening

When I heard the truck door slam, I turned again to look out the door, and to my surprise saw our milkman, Mr. Roberts, step up onto the schoolhouse porch. Teacher Leah left her second-grade class and went to the door to see what the visitor wanted.

Mr. Roberts had a baseball cap pulled down low over his face. He stood outside and leaned forward to peer in. I guess Teacher Leah thought he was too close to her, so she stepped back a bit. He looked sideways at the visitors, then held up a hitch-like kind of thing.

"Has anyone seen anything like this along the road?" His voice was low, and he kept shifting his eyes from one person to the next, then glancing at the floor as he spoke.

"Has anyone seen a clevis along the road?" Teacher Leah asked, turning to face us.

The boys shrugged their shoulders and several of us shook our heads slightly.

"Uh, can someone help me find it?"

Teacher Leah hesitated only a moment, then said, "Yes, some of the older boys could help you."

I saw Ammon and Joseph, the eighth-grade boys, wink at each other. They were more than willing to interrupt their lessons to help the neighbor man.

Mr. Roberts mumbled something, then turned around and left for his truck again. After watching him leave, Teacher Leah returned to her second-grade class.

After only a few minutes, I heard footsteps outside again. As I turned my head, I saw it was Mr. Roberts once more. He was carrying something in his right hand, and I knew right away it was not the clevis. It was a pistol! And it was pointed right at us!

He stepped inside and began waving it back and forth. "Everyone up front by the blackboard!" he ordered. His voice was stern, but still not loud or ominous.

I heard a sharp gasp from the visitors, but no one turned to look. All eyes were riveted on the gun.

"Come on! Everyone line up by the blackboards! Lie down on the floor, face down!" I could hear that he meant it, and to make sure we understood he was serious, he emphasized his words by waving the pistol.

The women in the back started forward, and as they reached our row of desks, we older ones hesitantly stood up and started forward as a group. Teacher Leah was already moving forward, the second graders clustered around her.

Our feet made shuffling noises on the tile floor as we moved toward the front, and I glanced anxiously at Hannah. Her eyes were wide as she looked at me beseechingly, but I had no look of comfort to give back to her. Several of us began squatting down on the floor. *Lie down?* That was the last thing I wanted to do!

I felt my eyes drawn back to Mr. Roberts. He was still standing in the back, waving his gun back and forth as we grouped together in the front. Then, with the gun still in his hand, he walked to the right side of the schoolroom and reached up to pull down the white window shade we used to keep the sun from shining into our faces. He pulled the blind down all the way, then walked toward the second window. When he pulled on the shade, the spring inside the roller snapped and the blind flipped up again. I jumped at the noise and felt a hard lump in my throat. I was now kneeling on the floor, but I craned my neck to see what was happening. "Lie down like he says," I heard one of the ladies say to us children. "Do just as he says!"

My heart was pounding rapidly, and I glanced at Teacher Leah for some kind of comfort. She and her mom were still not on the floor. I saw a look pass between them, then quickly, silently, Teacher Leah slipped out the side door.

Mr. Roberts had pulled the shade down again. When he turned back to face us, he must have realized someone had left. He waved his gun at us again and soon figured out that Teacher Leah was gone.

"Someone better go get her, or there will be trouble. Deep trouble!"

His gun was evidence that he was serious. We had very little time to analyze anything or to think about what might happen to us. Our minds were racing to make sense of what was happening and to figure out what to do.

Like a flash, a seventh-grade boy, Jacob, also slipped out the side door. I glanced back at Mr. Roberts to see what he would say or do. He was at the third window, pulling down that shade.

"You girls lie down!" he ordered again. "Heads toward the blackboard!"

There were eleven of us girls in school. From the two little first-grade girls, Martha and Joanna, all the way up to us eighth-grade girls.

There was a shuffling as we obeyed. I was on the right

side, closer to the side door. Hannah was first in line. Our other classmates were lined up between us. I don't know just where the boys were at that time, but the visitors were on the floor in a row just behind us. I could hear Mr. Roberts walking around, and I guess he was pulling down the shades on the other side of the room. He was talking to the boys, but I don't really know what he was saying. Then I heard the boys talking. Mr. Roberts must have left the room, but we didn't know it until he came back with some boxes and thumped them on the floor.

Sometimes people ask why we didn't run out the side door while we still had the chance. All I can say is that when a man has a gun and tells you what to do, you don't really think about disobeying—especially if you're already shocked and frightened.

Two-year-old Susie seemed to feel the tension, for she began to fret. I could sense her uneasiness as she wiggled restlessly in her mother's arms. I guess she was in an uncomfortable position.

"Put your feet up in the air!" Mr. Roberts was right behind us! I placed my head on my folded arms and slowly bent my knees.

I wanted so much to look around to see what he was doing, but another part of me wanted to keep my head hidden in my arms and not know what was happening. There were strange noises, as though a long board was being placed on the floor close to my head. Susie's fretting grew louder, and then baby Mose began crying. I wondered if Malinda still had him. I again heard Mr. Roberts talking and some other footsteps moving around. I heard the doors being closed, and I wondered what was going on.

I knew Mr. Roberts. He had been our milkman for several years now. True, I did not know him very well, for mostly he came late in the evening to pick up the milk from our dairy. The times I had seen him, he had not seemed unfriendly, just not outgoing or talkative. Quiet, mostly.

The scene from the evening before when he had been at our farm crept back into my mind. I remembered his few, terse words as he asked, "Will you hold this flashlight? I can't get this thing connected."

It had been dark in the milk house, and as the beam of light shone down on his hands, I had noticed that his fingers were clean, the nails trimmed short. I don't know why this came back to me now, but it did. Why was this quiet, tidy man doing this?

He was not acting like a crazy person. He wasn't screaming and yelling at us. He was talking in a normal voice, although you could hear that he meant what he said. He didn't seem angry or bitter.

I could hear someone else crying. It was little Martha, the blond-haired, blue-eyed first grader. I heard her quiet voice asking in Pennsylvania German, *"Vas dut ehr mit uns?"* (What is he doing with us?)

The sound of her quiet sobs, just up the row from me, tore into my heart. I realized how scared she must be. How scared all of us were.

Then little Mose began crying in earnest. Susie joined in, and the two children's loud sobs filled the schoolroom, echoing all of our feelings. I felt so helpless, so scared. Whatever was going to happen to us? What did Mr. Roberts want to do?

"All the women and their babies may leave," I heard Mr. Roberts say clearly. "Go on out!"

I heard a rustle as Malinda, Sylvia, and Lizzie got up off the floor. The crying children quieted somewhat as they were lifted into more comfortable positions.

A part of me wanted to protest. I had felt a little comfort in the fact that we were not alone. Teacher Leah had already left, and apparently her mother had slipped out as well. Now the other grownups were leaving too!

They must have left out the side door. I could hear baby Mose's cries diminish, then Mr. Roberts spoke again. "Boys, help me tie up the girls' feet."

Something inside of me shriveled when I heard those words. Tied up! My heart raced in panic. When the boys didn't respond, Mr. Roberts started down the line, binding each girl's feet. Then I realized something. There were only ten of us girls lined up! One was missing!

I went down the row in my mind. Hannah. Joanna. Martha. Lydia and Susan, the second graders. Yes, they were there. My sister Sadie Mae, Miriam, Ruth, Catherine, and Leona . . . Where was Leona? I went down the line again. I knew just where each one was. Leona was missing! Somehow she must have managed to slip out and escape!

I imagined how she must have felt as she slipped out the door, perhaps without Mr. Roberts even seeing her. He wouldn't remember how many students were in here, would he?

Where was Leona? Had she run away somewhere for help? I could feel myself in her shoes, running . . . where? Where would I go if I got out? Ah, yes! To Enos's place, just on the other side of the pasture next to Jacob's house. Surely someone there could help us.

I am not sure if I consciously began imagining what was happening outside to block out what was going on inside, but I knew Teacher Leah would do all she could to help us.

"All right, all of you boys, out!" Mr. Roberts said loudly. "Get!"

I could hear the shuffle of the boys' shoes as they obeyed. Then Mr. Roberts slammed the side door. I could hear him hammering something, and I turned my head and peeked at him. He was nailing boards across the side door, barricading anyone from coming in!

I looked straight into Hannah's eyes. The hurt, frightened look I saw in her face still haunts me. I wanted to say something, so I whispered, "We have to pray."

Beneath the cover of the banging hammer, I told some of the other girls, "We must pray! Please pray!"

"What are you girls doing?" Mr. Roberts stopped hammering and looked around. He must have heard us whispering.

"Praying," Hannah said calmly.

There was a mumble from Mr. Roberts, then he said, "Maybe you should pray for me."

"Why don't you pray too?" she replied. I marveled at Hannah's courage, yet I knew that was just like her.

"I don't believe in God anymore. I don't believe in prayer."

All was still for a moment, then he said, "If you let me do what I want, no one will get hurt."

I quickly said, *"Doonts net!"* (Don't do it!) loud enough for the rest of the girls to hear. I said it in Pennsylvania German so he wouldn't understand.

The Happening

Even though the uncomfortable position and the hard floor beneath me should have made the minutes seem like hours, I had no awareness at all of passing time. Sometimes people ask what all we thought about and if it seemed like we were in there for a long time, but I don't really remember. I really think part of the memory is gone, and at times when I talk with one of the other girls about what was going on in there, we remember things differently. We all are quite sure our version is right, but really, I think our minds were too bewildered by what was happening to take everything in.

I do know I was frightened and bewildered. Feelings I had never known to exist and didn't have names for went coursing through me. When my mind drifted to what evil things Mr. Roberts might do, I forced myself to think about other things.

I wondered what was happening at home. Had someone told my parents? I thought of dear little Rosie. Tears pricked my eyes and suddenly I wanted all this to be over. I wanted to be at home, around the table, like we had been that morning. I wanted the golden sunshine to wrap its warm arms around all of us. I wanted to be far, far away from this frightening, unknown place. I wanted to be with Teacher Leah and know all was well.

But here I was, lying face down on the schoolhouse floor by the blackboard, trying not to think. Trying to stay calm.

I prayed. Not with words, but just huge cries to God for help. I thought of the stories we had often heard at home and at church about the people in the early Anabaptist days who were persecuted because they believed in serving Jesus rather than obeying the rulers. I had often wondered how it must have been for those people, and had shuddered as I imagined the pain they must have felt as they were tortured. The preachers often said that the Christians felt the presence of God with them. That was what I wanted now.

And really, in spite of all the scariness, I could feel a certain calmness among us girls. Especially after we prayed. I clung to that.

Nobody will ever know just what all we felt there in our familiar schoolroom, in that weird and twisted situation. To be in this setting, without our teacher, without the normal classroom atmosphere . . . to be here with this man . . . Wasn't this our milkman, Mr. Roberts? No, this was a complete stranger. I no longer knew who he was.

I am just thankful that God let us feel His presence.

4

Pain and Confusion

Our legs were tied. We were still on the floor, trying to stay calm and praying—praying that God would be with us.

"I won't be home." I heard Mr. Roberts' voice and realized he was speaking on a cell phone. "Don't worry. I hear the police outside, and I want you to know that I am taking revenge for something that happened, uh, twenty years ago."

Nothing made sense, but my heart skipped a beat when I heard him say the police were outside. Someone must have called for help!

"I left notes for you and the children. Read them and you will understand. I won't be home again."

I could hear his footsteps cross to our side of the room. I knew he was standing right behind Hannah. Then I heard her protesting, "No! Stop it!"

I couldn't help but look. He had taken hold of her shoes. Suddenly we heard motors racing and car doors slamming.

I heard Mr. Roberts' cell phone beep three times as he dialed again, then the babble of a voice answering.

Mr. Roberts spoke clearly, "It's on White Oak Road. I just took . . ." his voice faltered, "ten girls hostage. I want everyone off the property or . . . or else." He spoke in a firm, normal tone.

I began to tremble as I heard him put it into words. There was another babble from the phone.

"Now!" There was more of an edge to his voice this time.

There was a brief pause, then he said, "Don't try to talk me out of it. Get 'em off the property, now!"

Another pause. "No, you tell them, and that's it. Right now, or they're dead—in two seconds."

I could hear some men talking outside. More and more noises surrounded the school, but inside all was quiet except for Mr. Roberts on the phone. "Two seconds—that's it!"

"Open up! Open up and come out!" A commanding voice from outside boomed into the silence.

Mr. Roberts walked toward the door. I could hear his footsteps plainly. Was he going outside? I felt a faint hope rising within me.

But the footsteps came back toward us, and my heart fell.

"I'm going to make you pay for what happened to my little girl!" His voice sounded weird now, almost strangled. "I'm sorry—I have to do it." Mr. Roberts spoke quietly, yet firmly, in his normal voice once more. "It's all because of what happened to my little girl, Eliza. Because of her."

Then a calmness settled over me. I didn't know what was going to happen, but in my heart I felt God was with me, and with all the other girls. I wanted to reach out and comfort my sister. I wanted to have some contact with my best friend Hannah. I longed to be able to gather little Martha close and whisper words of encouragement in her little ear. I could do none of those things. But I knew then that God could give comfort to each one of us girls, as He was giving me comfort.

How did I know he was going to shoot? I just felt it. That, and because of the racket outside, and all the warnings Mr. Roberts had given. I heard a click from his gun.

"Shoot me first," Hannah said calmly. "Shoot me and let the others go."

Then I heard Ruth's voice. "Shoot me next. Let the others go."

Most of us were crying quietly. I felt hot tears scorch my cheeks.

We heard a pounding on the double doors in the back. Something strong was being used! Would they rescue us?

Then the shooting started. Loud and sudden, the shots reverberated inside the schoolroom along with the cries and screams from us girls. Instantly I drew myself into a ball, trying to protect my face.

The sounds of gunfire and breaking glass, the impact of gunshot hitting my body, the sudden burst of policemen coming in through the windows and doors—all hit me as a huge wave of anguish, pain, and fear.

In the chaos that surrounded me, I tried to piece together what had happened. The deafening roar had stopped, and I was so thankful. Now a new sound filled the schoolhouse—people!

I know I did not faint, for I was dimly aware of strong arms lifting me and carrying me outside. Part of me was aware that it must be all over, and yet I did not want to leave without the other girls.

I was so grateful that I was no longer responsible for my own actions. I no longer had to hold myself together. I had no strength left—just this tremendous feeling that our ordeal was now over.

Maybe it was because I had been so keyed up and tense, but when those strong arms reached for me, I just gave myself up completely into their care. I did not know how hurt I was or if I could walk, but I knew something was wrong with my body. It did not seem to matter anymore. I was with someone I could trust.

My view of the man's jaw almost eye level with my head was unaccountably reassuring. Just the touch of someone who cared reduced my nerves to jelly. I felt hot tears pour from my eyes.

Then I was outside, and the warm sunshine was streaming onto my face. This abrupt change from the dim, surreal atmosphere inside was bewildering. How could the sun still shine? Why was the sky still blue? The policeman—I now recognized a uniform—stayed right with me. I could feel the strength of his arms tenderly cradling my spent body.

Then I was lying on the grass. The policeman called out to someone, and a woman hurried over. She knelt beside me, asking me questions.

"What is your name?" she asked, even as I felt her sure hands examining my painful side.

At first I could not answer. It did not seem important. I wanted to sit up.

"Just lie still! I'll help you." The woman's voice was kind, yet firm. It helped me to know someone was in control. Someone was responsible for me.

Beneath me, I could feel the grass against my cheek. For some reason, something so insignificant, yet so familiar, comforted me. My mind cleared and I heard myself say, "Rebecca Sue Lapp."

I felt someone tugging at the plastic bands that bound my feet together. In spite of the maddening pain that surged all through me, I felt immensely relieved to have my feet free, as though the rope that had tied me to the nightmare had been cut. I wanted to say, "Thank you," but I could not make myself talk.

My mind was in a whirl. There was so much activity all around me in the schoolyard. The police cars had their lights flashing, and it seemed like there were thirty or more people milling about. How had so many people come so quickly? My mind could not take it in. It drifted back . . .

What about the shooting? My sister! Hannah! All the girls I knew!

Then I became aware of the woman's voice again. She sounded young. "Are you allergic to any medicine that you know of?"

I shook my head, trying to focus on her face as she spoke.

"How old are you?"

"Thirteen."

I winced as I felt her firm hands touch a wound on my

side. "I know it hurts, honey, and I'm sorry, but I have to stop the bleeding."

Bleeding! How badly was I hurt?

"Can you tell me what happened?" she asked.

The question helped my mind focus instead of running wildly in all directions. Just what had happened?

"He tied us up. He shot us."

For a moment, the young woman looked away, then she looked into my face. "Did he do anything else? Did he touch you?"

"No. Only tied my feet." I wiggled my feet again to make sure they were free.

As the pain intensified, I realized that I had been shot. In the background I could hear people talking, and I strained to hear any of the voices of my classmates. But I heard none. I began to tremble violently.

I now realize that I was seeing the scene there in the schoolyard, yet was not really aware of what was going on. I distinctly remember seeing several of my classmates lying on the grass with people bending over them, and the constant moving of people around the yard. I saw the truck Mr. Roberts had come in. I saw the horse, still tied to the hitching rack. Even he looked scared at all the commotion. I could not shut out the noise—the calls from officials and the commands from people in charge. Every sound bounced around in my head.

Then I saw Joanna. She was sitting beside the white fence, and as I watched, she got up and began walking out the gate. Her face was dirty, and even at a distance I could see she looked bewildered. It did not seem strange to me that she began walking down the road toward the crossroads. I wanted to go home too. I wanted to leave this place with all its confusion and horror.

Someone must have seen her leave, for a medic hurried after the forlorn figure and brought her back to the schoolyard. Why couldn't we all go home?

More and more people arrived, and I was placed on a stretcher. I moaned in pain, but the hands that moved me were gentle. The young lady and the policeman stayed right beside me, talking to me in soothing tones.

Just before I was carried into an ambulance, as confused and pain stricken as I was, I saw something that impacted me deeply. A big, burly, uniformed policeman hung over the white board fence that surrounded our school, his body shaking with great, shuddering sobs.

Now I understand why, but right then, in my pain and shock, it made no sense. Was he hurt? Had he been shot? I often remember that scene, and it has helped me realize what those people who first arrived at our schoolhouse went through.

As they shut the ambulance doors, I remember hearing helicopters overhead. There were commands, people calling to each other, and orders from the policemen. Something horrible was happening. Had happened. Police . . . ambulances . . . helicopters . . .

I don't remember much about my ambulance ride. I do remember the nice woman telling me they were taking me to Lancaster General Hospital. All during the trip she kept talking to me, telling me what she was doing, and I was dimly aware of being poked with a needle. "This will prick as I put the needle into your arm, but it will help with the pain." I heard her talk to the driver, and the words, although meaningless to me, gave me a sense of comfort.

I have very little memory of arriving at the hospital. Mom tells me they checked me out there and decided to fly me to Hershey by helicopter. I think they must have given me some kind of medication that dulled my mind, for all of that part is a blur. It was so unreal. I didn't know any of the people around me. I was in and out of the ambulance, in and out of the helicopter, surrounded by voices.

Sedated or not, questions kept banging around inside my head.

What had happened to the rest of the girls?

Where was Sadie Mae?

What about Hannah and Catherine?

Little Martha?

There were also brief flashbacks of Mr. Roberts' voice.

"I'll make you pay for my little girl . . ."

"Sorry . . ."

". . . taken ten girls hostage."

I felt so weary. So drained and exhausted. Tired—that's what I was. Tired of the confusion that swirled around me. Tired of the haunting voices, and tired of the questions that had no answers. Suddenly all I wanted was my mother. I needed her desperately.

Hours must have passed, and yet I did not realize it. I was so used to people coming in and checking me at the hospital all that afternoon and into the evening that at first I didn't notice the small group filing into the room.

"Mom!" I cried out through the haze. Tears began streaming down my face. Finally I had what I had wanted all through this terrible happening. My mom! With her gentle, comforting hands stroking my face, the world that had been tipped crazily to one side began to right itself.

I saw my dad and felt his rough, strong hands stroke my hair. It took me a while to notice that Mom and Dad were not alone. Our neighbor, Teresa Dabney, was standing in the doorway, wiping her eyes. I assumed she had brought my parents all the way to the Hershey hospital.

It was so good to see people I knew! As kind as the nurses and doctors had been, just seeing my own people took away some of the pain in my head.

"Say hello to Mrs. Dabney," Mom said when she could control her shaky voice.

As Mrs. Dabney approached the bed, she knelt down on the floor and wrapped her arms around me the best she could. "You darling girl," she whispered through her tears. "We're all praying for you. I know God is with you."

I nodded my head. I couldn't speak.

Then I looked at my mom. I tried to read her face. She was sitting on a chair beside my bed just stroking my arm, her eyes fastened on her lap. I looked at Dad, standing behind her. His brown eyes were watching me, and in my father's face I could see at least some answers to my unspoken questions.

I still had to ask. "Is Sadie Mae all right?"

Mom's hand stopped its gentle caress and tightened. Then, clearing her throat, she looked at me through tears and said, "She went to heaven."

Heaven.

All of my short life I had heard about heaven. Whenever

I attended a funeral with my parents, the preachers always talked about heaven. In my mind, it was a place somewhere up in the sky where God and the angels lived. Where Jesus was. I was taught, and believed firmly, that all the innocent children who died went there. Plus all the people who had prepared themselves for the future—the ones who believed in God and in Jesus.

Now Sadie Mae was there. It seemed hard to grasp.

"I will never see her again." The words just tumbled out. I don't know where they came from.

My parents were both crying softly. It was Mrs. Dabney who was able to whisper, "No, Rebecca Sue, you will never see her on earth again. But remember, you will be able to see her when you get to heaven someday!"

Right then, I wanted to go. I wanted to leave this terrible happening, and a great longing to be with my little sister swept over me.

As if reading my mind, my dad said brokenly, "Daughter, we are so glad God spared you! At least we have you yet."

Then my mind began functioning. "Tell me! What about the others? Are they all dead too?" It was as though I was trying to prepare myself for the worst, lest my hopes would be dashed.

My mom shook her head. "We know almost nothing.

Except . . ." Then she could say no more as tears streamed down her cheeks.

Dad continued in a husky voice. "Little Martha, too, has passed away. But the rest . . . We waited all afternoon to hear what was happening, but we really know very little about the other girls."

"But why? How can you not know? Someone can tell you!" I was agitated. "If you know Sadie Mae and Martha are dead, why don't you know about the others?"

"Just try to relax," Mom told me kindly. "You shouldn't get yourself all worked up. We know several of the others are hurt, but we don't know how badly. You are all right, and we are here with you."

I nodded my head. I felt strange, not myself at all. Everything was so mixed up. I imagined Sadie Mae and Martha, floating away up to heaven, carried by the angels. A part of me was crying out against the pain, and a part of me was happy for the girls who were taken away from the horrible thing that had happened—that was happening.

Later, Mom told me it was probably the painkiller that made me feel all funny and impatient. I guess it does that to some people.

But one question would not go away. "Why did Mr. Roberts do this? How could he do this to us?"

I saw my dad's beard move up and down like it does when

he is moved deeply. "Rebecca Sue, no one knows why."

"He said he is sorry," I remembered. "He told us that he had to do it because of his little girl. Why did he?" I got all upset again as I remembered his words. Like a crashing wave of terror, my thoughts went back to what I had gone through.

The commotion. The loud noise. The roaring in the schoolhouse. Something about Mr. Roberts was tugging at my mind, but my brain seemed incapable of grasping what it was. It was as though I knew what had happened to him, but still, I did not know. I wanted to ask, but I felt my breath come in quick, short gasps. I needed air . . .

"Let's not talk about it now," Mom said, her lips in a firm line. *"Sei ruich!"*

Be restful. I had heard this phrase all my life. Not only did it mean be restful in our bodies, but also in our spirits. I willed myself to obey.

Soon a nurse came in and gave me a shot. Both of my parents stayed with me until I dozed off. I awoke several times during the night and pushed aside the haze long enough to make sure my mother was still in the chair beside me. I knew something terrible had happened in my life, but as long as my mom was still there, I did not have to allow the vague shapes in my troubled mind to have faces.

5

The Funeral

"Do you want some orange juice?" I remember my dad's words rousing me from somewhere I had slipped off to.

Looking past him, I realized I was in a strange place. I saw a long plastic tube reaching down from a plastic bag hanging above my head. Oh, yes—the hospital. My mind started reeling . . . trying to remember . . . something had happened . . . What day was this? I knew it was daytime, because I could see the sun shining in through the window.

I looked back at my father's face. He was holding a glass of orange juice toward me, the straw conveniently bent so I could drink without having to sit up. The cold juice felt refreshing to my throat. I shifted in bed and felt pain surge through me. I winced and tried to hold still.

"Well, how is my patient this morning?" I turned. The cheerful voice belonged to a doctor who had just entered my room. "You have come through your surgery nicely. Now you just need to rest and heal." Turning to my dad, he spoke kindly, "Sir, your daughter is doing quite well." He studied the chart in his hand, then added softly, "We are all deeply moved by what you have gone through."

"Thank you." My dad's voice was not quite steady. "We must be thankful to God that it was not worse."

The doctor stared at my dad, then looked at me. "Yes, yes," he stammered hastily. "I guess you're right, but I don't think I could say that just now if I were in your shoes."

As he was leaving, I heard him mutter, "Amazing!"

What were they talking about? Then my mind flew back to the happening of the day before. I could still hear the crunch of the truck tires on the gravel when Mr. Roberts arrived, then his muffled voice talking to Teacher Leah. I relived the scene of him pulling the blinds, the women leaving, the boys leaving, and then . . . my mind jumped to the schoolyard after it was all over. Me lying outside, and the medic asking, "What is your name?"

Mr. Roberts . . . My mind was not at rest. Something about Mr. Roberts. I knew something, didn't I? But not quite.

"Dad?" I half whispered. "Where is Mr. Roberts?"

I felt my father's hand stroke my hair. "He does not live," he said simply.

He was dead. I had known that. I must have realized it even in the schoolroom, before I was carried out. But now I had heard it spoken, and for me, it was real.

Sadie Mae! Like swiftly flying darts, my thoughts flew to my younger sister. She had died! Died, and gone to heaven!

In my mind I could see her running over the lawn that morning, her puppy, Roxie, bounding along behind. I could still see the golden sunlight pouring over the scene, turning everything into light and laughter. Her laugh echoed in my mind.

"Why did he do it?" I heard myself asking. "Oh, why did he do it?"

"We don't know," Dad said softly, his voice husky. "He must have been a very unhappy man. As hard as it is, God wants us to forgive him."

"And Martha is dead too," I remembered out loud. "Tell me, Dad . . ."

I didn't ask the questions that were beginning to form inside my head just then. I saw my mom coming into the room, and my grandparents behind her. At the sight of them, tears stung my eyelids. I don't know what all they said, but it was comforting beyond words to see them. There was something familiar in this strange place after all.

Then more people came in. I saw Emma, little Martha's mother. Through her tears, she smiled at me and placed her hand on my forehead. I could not help but cry with her. Martha had been their only daughter. Now they only had boys in the family.

Then I was left alone with my mother. Silence settled in the room.

"Mom," I tried out my voice. "What happened . . . what happened to the others?"

It was then that I heard the shocking and tragic news. Besides my sister and little Martha, Hannah had died. My best friend! Ruth had also gone to heaven, along with her sister Susan. Miriam was still alive, but in critical condition.

Catherine, Lydia, and Joanna were all wounded and in the hospital, though not all in the same one. Joanna and Catherine were in the children's hospital in Philadelphia. Lydia was in Hershey Medical Center. It took a moment for me to realize that I, too, was in Hershey. So I was with Lydia, in a way . . .

"Mom! I wish . . ." I broke off my sentence, for there, coming in the door, was Teacher Leah!

My head began to swim. I was glad I was lying down. I closed my eyes as I felt her arms cradle my head close to her. Tears streamed down onto my pillow. My pent up emotions broke loose and I cried and cried, ignoring the pain in my side. I could feel my teacher's frame shaking as she cried with me.

When the tears slowed, she handed me a handkerchief and I dried my eyes. "Rebecca Sue, remember, God loves you very much, and He cares about you! He knows just how much you hurt inside. Jesus suffered all His pain and death so He can comfort us in our sorrow."

That's how our teacher is. She knows just the right words to say, and they're not empty words. She knows what she's talking about. I can feel it.

The following days were a blur. Nurses. Doctors. People in and out. The second day, my parents brought my little sister Rosie to see me. Elam and Benuel came along too, with Mommi and Dawdi. We were all together. No, not quite all together. Sadie Mae was missing. "But maybe she can look down from heaven and feel with us," my grandmother said comfortingly.

Rosie seemed awed by the room, and at first she clung tightly to my mother. Before they left, she did give me a hug.

I wanted to cling to her tightly, but I knew it was all too strange for her. It was too strange for me too.

"Friede sei mit eich! (Peace be unto you.) As Jesus said, 'My peace I give unto you,' so may we have the peace of God in our hearts this morning," the preacher's voice rang clear and strong.

"This may seem a strange way to address you in this situation, but Jesus has come to give us peace—peace in our hearts. As we gather together this morning, we need to be thankful to God that He has granted His mercies and loving-kindnesses to us once more."

I had answered without hesitation when my parents had asked me if I felt strong enough to attend Sadie Mae's funeral. Now, from my padded chair, I had a clear view all around the big shop where the funeral service was being held. I was with my family, close to the front. Close to the casket that held my sister's body.

"We know that, like this little girl lying before us, we will all die someday." The words went winging over the crowd all around me. I glanced to the right and saw rows of young girls, women, and children sitting on backless benches, all dressed in black, as is the Amish custom. The young boys and the men sat on the left side. In the center section, where

I was, were my relatives—my grandparents, uncles, aunts, and many cousins.

"As God has forgiven us, so we must forgive others." The words the preacher spoke were plain and easy to understand. "When we pray the Lord's Prayer, we say, 'Forgive us our debts, as we forgive our debtors.' These are more than just words. They must be a reality for all Christians! Perhaps we think we have a choice in the matter. But we are actually asking God not to forgive us if we do not forgive others. This is serious!"

As he continued to talk about forgiveness, I searched deep down in my heart. Had I forgiven Mr. Roberts for what he had done? I remembered what my father had told me when I had asked about Mr. Roberts—"God wants us to forgive him." Now I thought about that. My dad was willing to forgive the man who had killed his daughter, my sister! Deep in my heart, I knew that I, too, must forgive.

"It is easy to forgive when someone says he is sorry and asks us to forgive." The preacher's voice broke through my thoughts again. "But what if the person who does the wrong never asks our forgiveness? What then?"

The entire congregation was silent. I heard the whimper of a baby in his mother's arms.

The words came clearly and simply. "We must still

forgive. There is no question. As Jesus forgives our sins and our mistakes, so we must forgive others. All others."

I thought about Mr. Roberts' family. He had lived just down the road in Georgetown, barely two miles from our school. His wife and their three young children still lived there. I wondered where his widow was this morning. What was going through her mind? Did she know why her husband had done this? How terrible life must be for her!

". . . hard on us to see innocent children suffer." I paid attention to the preacher again. "It is almost harder for us to bear the thought of those who are hurt than those who are no longer with us."

A lump rose in my throat. I thought of the other girls who were still in the hospital. I thought of Miriam, who Mom had told me was still in very serious condition. I thought of Catherine and Lydia and Joanna. I wondered how many more would die.

". . . that special place in heaven for all the children who die is big enough for the ones who were taken away from us. We have this comfort and assurance from God."

I could hear people crying softly. I did not dare look around, for I knew it would hurt to see the emotion on people's faces.

I eased myself into a slightly different position. Someone

had kindly placed cushions on my wheelchair, and I could lean back to rest. The ambulance that had brought me was waiting outside to take me back to the hospital after the funeral.

The second preacher was not from Lancaster County. I could tell because he was dressed differently, and when he spoke, his Pennsylvania German dialect was different too. Yet he spoke plainly and simply, and even we children could understand.

"We are born sinners," I distinctly remember him saying, "and we will die sinners, unless we do something about it. Unless we believe in Jesus Christ and ask Him to forgive our sins and make us His children. Then we will not die sinners, but as people saved by grace and mercy—the grace and mercy of God."

At times he spoke English. I knew it was for the benefit of the non-Amish who were sitting in the back. I had not seen them all clearly, but I knew they were there at the invitation of my family. I had noticed the Dabneys among them, and Teresa had waved at me.

I wondered what they thought of our service. I didn't know if they had ever been at an Amish funeral before. Perhaps they thought it strange that no songs were sung. This is our tradition. For regular Sunday church, we sing in German, of course, but at funerals there is no singing at all.

When the long funeral service ended, people began filing past the casket to view my sister's body for the last time. Many had been at our house the night before to comfort my family, but they had come today too. As the line filed past in front of me, I got to see people I had not seen since the happening. I watched as the boys from our school walked past the black homemade casket. I could see they were deeply moved as they saw my sister for the last time.

"It's only Sadie Mae's body," I reminded myself when, at the end, our family went forward. Elam wheeled my chair so I could see my younger sister's face. She looked like she was peacefully sleeping. We cried together as a family and said our silent goodbyes.

Then we drove to the cemetery. As our buggy turned at the crossroads in Georgetown, I could hardly believe my eyes! There were cars and vehicles and news reporters all along the road! Everywhere I looked, I saw more and more people. I had heard my family talking about all the news reporters who had come to Nickel Mines and how the firehouse in Georgetown was swarming with people, but I had never imagined just how crowded our peaceful countryside had become!

"Mom, just look!" I gasped. I pointed to a pair of policemen on horseback who rode ahead, leading our funeral procession of horses and buggies. Then I pointed to the crowds of strangers lining the road. Many held cameras.

"Yes, people are very curious," Mom responded curtly. "I just wish they would leave us alone."

"I hope that somehow people will turn their hearts toward God through all this," my father's steady voice reminded us. "We don't like it, but people are always curious."

Then we reached the cemetery. The buggy carrying the coffin stopped outside the fence, and our family gathered once more for the final viewing. This one was the hardest, for it was our last glimpse of dear little Sadie Mae. I cannot tell you much about that scene. It was too painful.

After the burial, people stopped to talk to us. I realized that some of the English people who were there must have been at the school during the happening. Several spoke to me, and I saw tears in their eyes as they shook my hand. One young lady put her arms around my mother. I wondered if she was the one who had taken care of me. Or maybe the one who had cared for Sadie Mae.

I had not realized until then how many of the community people had been deeply affected. Before, I had thought it was only our own people's hurt and grief. Now I saw that it was the agony of our entire community. Only later would I realize how far away, even in foreign countries, the happening had touched people's hearts.

All the way back to the hospital, I tried to remember the preacher's words. Whenever I had to fight back the tears that wanted to come as I thought of my sister, my friends who had died, or the ones hurt and wounded in the hospitals, I made myself think of the words I had heard that morning: "Trust in God. Bring your cares to Jesus. Don't ask why—just allow God to carry all your burdens."

I did find comfort. I sensed that God was guiding us all through this terrible time, and that somehow He still loved and cared for us. In that I could rest.

6

More Questions

About three weeks after the happening, the doctors said I was ready to go home. Though my parents had prepared me concerning many things while I was in the hospital, I knew it would be difficult to face the reality of my new life.

Mom had told me the schoolhouse had been torn down. But now, driving home, I wondered what I would find.

"What does it look like now?" I asked.

"What?" Mom asked, startled from her own thoughts.

"The school."

She looked at me for a long time before answering.

"The schoolhouse is gone," she told me again. "It's now a meadow, and there's not a trace of anything left. Only the maple trees are still there."

Funny how such a small detail triggered a flood of memories. The maple trees. In warm weather, we girls often sat under the spreading branches of a maple tree to eat our lunches, while the boys sat under the tree on the other side of the schoolhouse. During my first several years in school, we younger ones would sometimes play house around the trunks of the trees. Cradling imaginary babies, we would try to imitate the cries of little children, then shush them like we had seen our mothers do in church and at home. At times, if we could persuade the boys to participate, we would get one to "preach" to us, his voice rising and falling like a real preacher's.

The schoolhouse, too, held many memories—memories of cold winter days when we would rush inside after our walk to school and crowd around the heater . . . of hanging our coats on the hooks, each marked with a name to keep order. Everything was familiar, and life was orderly and stable.

Mom waited patiently for the questions she knew would come. "Mom," I asked, "why did the school board decide to tear down the schoolhouse?"

With a quick shake of her head, Mom answered. "Every time I went past there and saw the schoolhouse all quiet and the windows boarded up, I had to turn my head the other way. There are too many memories, and that's the way the rest of the Amish feel too. It is our practice to erase bad things and move on with life. Getting rid of the schoolhouse was one of the best ways to do this."

I guess I had blocked out much of the happening, because for me, when I thought of the school, I still remembered the happy times of earlier days. The schoolhouse surrounded by the white board fence was a special place for me. Or it had been a special place. Now it was gone.

"If we can rid ourselves of things that remind us of what happened, we can better get on with life," Mom repeated, though she was looking out the window when she said it, more like she was telling herself than talking to me. "I wish I could wash myself of all bad memories."

The hard lump inside me seemed to grow again. I wondered if, from now on, I would always have this weight inside me, pushing down on my chest, pushing down on my life.

With great effort, I willed myself to think of something else. I looked out the van window toward the horizon, where the gray sky met barren cornfields.

Finally the driver turned off the road and we started up the lane to our farm. We had not driven through Nickel

Mines, so I did not have to see where our schoolhouse had been. I was not ready for that yet. I think my parents knew that.

It was hard enough to come home. Would it be home without Sadie Mae? I wanted to return, yet a part of me wanted to stay in the hospital, where another world had become at least familiar enough to make me dread coming home to face life without my sister.

As we pulled into our lane, my grandparents walked out the front door of their side of the house. I saw Elam look out the door of the woodworking shop, then run down behind the house, probably to wash his hands. So typical of Elam, who is always careful to stay as clean and neat as possible. Whether at work in the shop or doing even dirtier work on the farm, my brother always makes sure he is clean when he comes into the house.

Just that familiar scene made the lump in my chest swell, for I realized how normal life really was. Yes, things had changed, and yet many things were still the same. The farm was the same, our house was still in the same place, and even though the shade trees were losing their leaves and the yard needed to be raked, this was home!

"Rebecca Sue! Welcome home!" My grandmother's kind, gentle face beamed at me. Roxie bounced around, barking at all the excitement.

Seeing Sadie Mae's little dog sent a sharp pain through me, but I tried to push any sad thoughts away. I even laughed a little as her wet tongue licked my hand. "She still remembers me!" I told my family.

Inside the house there was a banner someone, probably Benuel, had made, spelling out, "Welcome Home, Sister!" My big brother liked to draw, and he often spent his evenings illustrating Bible verses or poems. Bouquets of flowers brightened the rooms, and I saw a basket of unopened greeting cards on the floor beside the sofa.

Not till I was settled on the couch in the living room did it seem Rosie could finally accept me as her big sister. She had been clinging to Mom's dress, but now she nestled up to me on the sofa. I held her hungrily against my good side, and her small head felt so good against my cheek. She was now my only little sister. Somehow she had to fill Sadie Mae's place.

I was tired, and Mom covered me with a light blanket, even though it was not cold. The blanket felt comforting, and I drifted into a nap, very conscious of finally being at home again. I did not dare think of who was missing.

Just before my eyes closed, I saw Elam peeking around the corner of the door. He saw me looking at him, and he winked his special wink and smiled. I tried to smile back. A warm feeling spread over me. I was home!

"There were people everywhere," Elam told me, shaking his head. "It was like a Sunday, except people were dressed in their everyday clothes. More and more people came until the lane was blocked with vehicles and horses were tied up all along the fence."

It was evening, and I had eaten my fill of Mom's good cooking. She had fixed a plate and brought it to me in the living room, because I was still too sore to move around much.

Now everyone else had gone outside, except Elam.

In spite of our different natures, Elam and I are very close. I have always admired his quick ways, so much like Mom and . . . Sadie Mae. Or like Sadie Mae was. Elam talks a lot and makes friends wherever he goes. He likes to play volleyball and is often chosen quickly, sometimes even before some of the older boys. Plus, he is a great tease and loves to play practical jokes.

"When did you get there?" I asked. "How did you find out?"

Elam stared at the wooden floorboards for a moment. Then he looked at me and asked, "Are you strong enough for this talk? Maybe it would be better not to talk about it right now."

I shook my head. "I want to know."

Nodding his head, he said, "I knew there would come a time when you would ask. I know you well, sister.

"Anyway, I was working in the shop with Dad. All at once we heard a pickup truck coming in the lane in a terrible hurry. It was our neighbor, Mr. Brown. Right away we both knew something awful must have happened, and we ran down to the front of the house to wait on him.

" 'Get in right away! Something terrible has happened at school!' he shouted to us.

"Mom had run out onto the porch, and Mommi and Dawdi had rushed out onto their porch. 'What is it?' Mom yelled.

" 'There's a man at the schoolhouse with a gun, and he kept the girls!' I remember trying to figure out what he was saying.

"Mom and Dad jumped into the truck and Mr. Brown sped away. Dawdi told me to hitch up the horse, then Mommi came out of the house with Rosie and we all hurried over to the farm."

I knew which farm he meant—the Jacob Stoltzfus farm. The land where the schoolhouse had stood. The back of the big dairy farm, towering against the sky with huge barns and tall silos, had been the backdrop for our schoolyard. A farm pond reflected the blue sky and floating white clouds on fair days.

Elam shook his head. "No one seemed to know what was happening. I saw Teacher Leah talking to some people, and I could see she had been crying. Her parents were there, and the parents of the other school children.

"Then I saw the boys from school. They were sitting in a row in front of a shed, saying nothing. Several of them kicked at the gravel in front of them. When I saw Ammon, I went over and asked him what was happening. He's the one who told me what was going on—at least what he knew."

I listened as Elam's tale unfolded. I relived the first moments when Mr. Roberts had entered the schoolroom. Through Ammon's eyes, and through Elam's retelling, the long minutes of that hour unfolded once again.

Suddenly I realized how little time all this had taken. It had all happened in less than an hour! Mr. Roberts had first come into our school at 10:25. An hour later, I was in an ambulance on the way to the hospital. And Sadie Mae was dead.

The boys had not known what to do when they were first released. First they clustered together behind the boys' outhouse. When they saw the women motioning to them from the pasture, they hurried across the meadow toward the farm. On the way up, they saw Jacob and his son-in-law Enos running out from behind the girls' outhouse, looking toward the schoolhouse. The truck Mr. Roberts had borrowed from his wife's grandfather, Mr. Welk, was still parked in front of the schoolhouse. The horse and buggy the women had driven to school that morning was still tied up. The schoolhouse, shades drawn, looked deserted.

"Ammon said the boys were already at the farm when Mr. Roberts began shooting. They watched the police cars rush in, then they heard the shots. That was about eleven o'clock. I remember how white and scared his face looked as he told me." Elam's face showed his own emotion.

"Where was Teacher Leah?" I wanted to know. "And Leona?"

Elam shook his head. "I didn't see them right then. So many people were milling around, and more people kept coming. Even though it was kind of quiet and subdued, it was still bewildering. I remember noticing that one of our women was hugging an afghan around her and shivering, even though it was warm and sunny. No one knew what was happening, but we all knew it was something terrible."

I again thought of that horrendous day. I remembered how Hannah had so bravely said, "Shoot me first. Let the others go." But I could not talk about that. I wanted to know more about what had happened at the farm. "How did the police find out what was happening?"

"Teacher Leah had run up to the farm and dashed into Enos's house yelling, 'Call 9-1-1! There's a man with a gun at the school!' Enos ran outside to the telephone shanty and called."

Ah! So that's where Teacher Leah had gone when she had slipped out the side door. She had gone for help. I swallowed the growing lump in my throat.

Just then Mom came in carrying Rosie. She looked over at Elam and me, then went into the bathroom to wash up my baby sister.

"What happened next?" I asked. I wanted to know more. I needed to fill in the gaps in my mind.

Elam shook his head. "I hardly know. I remember many of the grownups went inside the house. Someone said they were praying. We could see people gathering across the road from the schoolhouse, and there were many police cars with flashing lights. Then ambulance sirens started wailing. I felt frustrated and helpless, because I didn't know where you and Sadie Mae and the other girls were. We didn't know if you were all right or not. It was horrible!"

I heard Dad come in from the side porch. Water splashed as he washed in the sink.

"Elam," he called.

Elam followed Dad, and I was left alone in the growing darkness. All was silent, except for the mantle clock ticking steadily on the shelf. I could hear the murmur of voices as Dad talked with Elam. Then the door slammed, and I heard Benuel's voice. He must have been working late, for he had not been home for supper. Mom had kept food warm for him, and I was glad when he came into the living room with his plate.

"Welcome home, Rebecca Sue." His quiet, steady voice told me how glad he was to see me. "I missed you."

Tears wanted to wash my eyes once more, but I swallowed hard and nodded. I knew he would know how I felt. Benuel and I were the quiet ones, taking in much but leaving the talking to Mom, Elam, and Sadie Mae. But Benuel and I were more like Dad.

Or I had been that way. Right then, I didn't know how I was. At times after the happening, I found myself chattering away when visitors came to see me. Other times I hardly knew what to say. I was not sure just who I was anymore. The miserable pressure building up inside my chest was changing me into someone else.

"Where were you when you heard about it?" I asked Benuel. I had a burning desire to know how other people found out—what they did and how they responded.

"My boss on the carpentry crew heard something on his scanner. He's on the Gap Volunteer Fire Department, so he hears the calls on his radio." Benuel's fork clinked against his plate.

Mom came downstairs after putting Rosie to bed, and Dad and Elam joined us in the dark living room.

"Rebecca Sue, don't you think you need to sleep now?" Dad's voice was kind. "It may not be good for you to be talking so much."

I could feel the pressure inside me. "I want to know, Dad," I said softly. "I don't know why, but I have all these questions."

"We understand," Mom said quickly. "But for tonight, this is enough."

I nodded obediently.

That first night at home was uneventful. It felt so good to be at home! As sleep swept me away into the night, I felt as though I was carried on arms of love. In spite of everything, God seemed very near.

Three days later, when I was feeling well enough to wander slowly around the house, I saw something else that etched itself into my mind.

I had not been upstairs since my return home, so I began climbing the stairs slowly, one step at a time, like a little child, holding onto the banister. I reached the top and saw Mom in the bedroom I used to share with Sadie Mae and Rosie. She was on her knees in front of the bureau where our clean clothes were stored. The bottom drawer was open, and beside her on the wood floor I saw stacks of Sadie Mae's clothes, neatly folded. Mom must have washed them, and now she was putting them away, perhaps until Rosie was old enough to wear them.

But it was my mother's expression that held my attention. A look of pain and suffering was spread across her face, and I was startled to see my mother like this. I felt like I was intruding.

I turned and tiptoed down the stairs. I could not bear to let my mother know I had seen her.

When she came back downstairs, there was no trace of the expression I had seen earlier. "Oh, look at the time! I must make dinner for the men. They will be in soon," she fussed, and immediately set about fixing our meal.

Our dinner is in the middle of the day. Sure, Mom cooks good food for supper too, but we are used to having the main meal at noon on the farm.

"When did you find out Sadie Mae was gone and I was at the hospital?" The same burning questions just ran around and around in my head. I looked at Elam, trying to find answers.

We sat outside on the porch swing on a Sunday afternoon. Even though October was almost over, this afternoon the sun warmed us.

"Mom said we should not talk about it so much," Elam said, pushing against the porch floor with his shoe. "It might not be good for you."

I thought about it. Yes, there was a part of me that did not want to know. A part of me wanted to go on with life and forget what had happened. But a bigger part of me had to know more. It was like a dark hole inside of me I just had to fill. My mind could not rest until I did.

"Oh, no!" Elam mumbled. Following his gaze, I saw a big van pull into our lane.

Visitors. Again.

"I'm out of here." Elam got up abruptly and dashed inside. I could hear him running upstairs.

I didn't want to be outside by myself, so I followed him inside. I sat down in the living room. The flow of voices, first outside on the lawn, then coming into the house, washed over me. I looked at the curious faces and tried to be polite as the strangers crowded inside and asked questions. I heard my parents answer and try to satisfy the strangers' curiosity about the happening. When they asked me how I felt, I replied, *"Goot"* (fine), like usual. Really, about the only thing I felt anymore was numbness whenever visitors came. They had come every day since I'd been home. Or at least it sure seemed like it.

"We don't know why God allowed it to happen, but we know He will take us through any pain and suffering," Teresa Dabney said softly, sitting beside me on her sofa.

I had asked Mom if I could go see our neighbors one evening, and Teresa had welcomed me with open arms.

I nodded my head in agreement. "I know God is with us all." I felt my eyes brim with tears as her kindness enveloped me.

Teresa dabbed her own eyes with a tissue. "Your family is so strong. I can see that your faith in God is taking you through this terribly difficult time. That is so wonderful!"

Then we talked about other things. She got a mail order catalog and showed me what flowers she was going to order to plant next spring. She asked which ones I liked, and I found I could even bear talking about how Sadie Mae had enjoyed helping with her outside work.

Then Mr. Dabney came home. When he saw me sitting on the couch with his wife, he walked on into the kitchen, and when he returned with a cup of coffee, his eyes looked red. But we all talked together pleasantly.

The time came to say goodbye, and I headed for the door. I had been able to forget about the happening, at least for a while, but now, as I returned to my own home, I felt guilty for having had a good time.

"When did you find out one of your daughters had been killed?" I could hear the woman's voice downstairs questioning Mom. She had driven in unexpectedly while all the men were gone and had started talking to Mom in the kitchen.

"Well," Mom said simply, "when I was at the farm."

"Would that be the Jacob Stoltzfus farm?" the woman prodded helpfully.

Mom must have nodded, for the next question came right away.

"What kind of emotions did you experience?"

"Well, I was all shook up, of course." I could hear my mom warm up a little, as we children would tease her about doing when she got started talking. "I wanted to head over to the schoolhouse right away to see for sure if it was my daughter. But the police would not let any of the parents go down there. They said it was too terrible. So some of our preachers went."

"What did they say? When they came back, I mean."

"They told us it was our Sadie Mae and little Martha who had died at the scene. I kept asking, 'What about Rebecca Sue?' But no one had any answers. None of us knew how the rest of the girls were. That was hard."

"Now what is your name again? Oh, yes, that's right—you don't want to give your name. That's all right. It's rather difficult to keep everyone straight with so many involved, you know. Plus, so many same names, and everyone dressed alike. Now let me get it straight. You don't have any bitterness or bad feelings against Mr. Roberts or his family?"

"Ma'am," Mom's voice showed deep feeling, "we are not perfect. We do struggle with questions and feelings, but in the Bible God tells us we are to forgive. So we have forgiven Mr. Roberts, even though he is not alive, and hold nothing against him or his poor widow and family. Our hearts go out to her, and we want to do anything we can to help her."

After a brief pause, the woman said, "I hear that the Amish went to Mr. Roberts' funeral. Were you there?"

"No," Mom explained, "I was in the hospital with my daughter."

"And she is doing well?"

"We feel she is doing as well as can be expected. We are thankful to God for the healing He has given to all the girls."

"Even to Miriam? I understand she's just a vegetable."

Mom's voice rose. "No one is just a vegetable! Yes, God has even done miracles with Miriam. The doctors sent her home to die, but she still lives. We know God can still heal her."

"Well, thank you for your time," I heard the woman say. I wondered if she realized my mother was upset by her last comment. "It sure must be hard on you folks, so gentle and quiet, to have something horrible like this happen to you. It was so uncalled for, and now the whole world knows about it."

Then the door closed, and it was quiet inside our house. I heard the van drive away.

"Listen to this," Elam announced two days later as he marched into the house carrying the daily paper.

" 'I was all shook up and wanted to rush right down to try to identify my daughter,' one of the mothers said, 'but the police would not allow us to, and I felt I was falling apart inside. I did not know what to do,' continued the mother, who did not want to give her name. 'It was a terrible time for us. We tried hard to trust in God.' "

He continued to read, " 'This Amish woman, seated in her parlor, was dressed in the simple blue clothes that married

Amish women wear. Her hair was parted in the middle and a white cap adorned her head.' "

Elam shook his head in disgust and threw the paper on the floor. "Why do they do it? They try to make us look as weird as they can."

"I was not in the parlor," Mom interrupted, picking up the paper. "I was right here in the kitchen. We don't even have a parlor! We have a living room like everyone else."

"Mom!" Elam exclaimed, turning to face her. "This woman—this reporter who wrote this article—was here?"

"Now, Elam," Dad said quietly. "Your mother has told me about it, and we will not blame her. She already feels bad about the whole thing."

Elam was breathing rapidly. "I am so sick and tired of all the hoopla! Reporters snooping around, trying to interview our people, trying to find out what makes us tick! Don't they realize we are people, with real emotions and feelings? Just because we look different and live different lifestyles doesn't make us into some kind of exotic animal! I'm sick and tired of it! In the news, in the paper, all over! Remember those women who tried to get into Hannah's funeral? Tried to slip in as Amish, and it was as plain as daylight they weren't Amish! One was even dressed in pink! For a funeral! It was . . ."

Dad is often slow to speak, but this time he interrupted

Elam's tirade. "Son, I know how you feel, and you are probably right about many things. We must be fair, however, because there have also been many sympathetic and kind news reporters. As hard as it is to realize, this happening is not only our happening. It has touched the lives of thousands outside our community. Many are grieving along with us, and they genuinely want to help and uplift us. Many are praying."

Elam didn't say anything, and soon found an excuse to go upstairs.

"I think we've talked about this enough," Mom said. "Rebecca Sue, it's time for you to go to bed."

7

Shadows

A man crept stealthily around the corner. His face was hidden by shadows. His movements were slow and deliberate; his steps made no sound. I could feel my entire body stiffen, and I wanted to run, but my feet would not obey my will. I was frozen to the spot.

Closer and closer, the man loomed ever larger. I gathered all my strength and tried to scream. My heart seemed to burst right out of my chest.

Then I awoke, and the morning light was shining into my bedroom window through the now bare maple branches. My heart was racing and my breath came in short gasps. The pain I had felt in my dream did not go away, and I could feel a weight deep inside me—the weight that was always present and some days seemed to smother me.

I turned my head on the pillow and was reassured to see Rosie's sweetly sleeping face next to me. At least my bad dream had not awakened her.

This had not been the first dream since the happening, but it had been the most vivid. I knew who the man was, even though in my dreams his face had been hidden in the dark. I shivered, drawing myself up into a ball and hiding my face in the pillow. Then I quickly straightened again as I remembered how I had drawn myself up to escape the bullets.

"Rosie!" I whispered. "Do you want to see the morning?" I had to say something out loud to someone—to do something normal that might bring me back to real life.

I shook my little sister. Slowly she opened her eyes and looked at me. Then her forehead wrinkled and she turned away and whimpered, nestling deeper under the blankets. I turned toward the window, disappointed, and a feeling of despondency settled over me.

Later, after breakfast, I was going through some of the cards. There were boxes full of them from people all over the world. Many people had written notes of encouragement and sympathy. Hardly any of the names were familiar, but it helped pass the time to read the postmarks and see how far the news had spread.

It was all somewhat bewildering to me. Why were so many people interested in what had happened to us here in Nickel Mines? We were just a small, quiet community of normal people, living and working and going to school like people all over Lancaster County. We were not in the heavily advertised part of Amish Country, like along Route 30 where tourists clogged the roads and signboards directed visitors to the local places of interest. We were tucked away behind a ridge, in our own place with rolling hills and open farms. But now we were suddenly thrown into national—even international—attention. All because of that man.

"Mom," I asked when she passed through the living room, "why do you think he did it?"

Mom poured some water from a pitcher around the African violets on the windowsill. She turned them so the back sides of the plants would get more light. I watched her pinch off a yellowed leaf. Hadn't she heard me?

"That is a question I don't think will ever be answered," she finally said. Her voice was strained, and I realized she was trying to stay calm. "I ask the same question myself over and over. I am sure his widow, Marie, is asking the same question."

Suddenly she was beside me, and we were crying together. It felt good to share my grief with my mom. But the weight inside me did not go away.

I think it was that same evening, before I went upstairs to bed, that Dad came over to where I was listlessly turning the pages of a book. Benuel was the only other person in the room.

"Rebecca Sue," he began gently, "Mom says you are still asking why the man . . . why Mr. Roberts did what he did. Is it bothering you often?"

I could not speak. I just nodded my head.

"No one seems to know just what made him do what he did." Dad stopped for a moment. "If this upsets you, we don't have to talk about it."

I could barely whisper, but I said, "I want to know, please."

"He left notes for his wife and children, saying he was doing this because he was so angry at God for taking his baby girl away when she was only several days old. He also mentioned some other troubling things, but nothing that really makes sense.

"Many who knew him said he was just an ordinary man, though really quiet. He seemed to love his children and wife, but somehow, something happened."

"What makes people do things like that? How can they be normal?" I heard doubt in my own voice.

"It can be bitterness, or unforgiveness," Dad explained. "Perhaps he knew he had sin in his life and was not willing to repent. If we let small sins remain in our hearts, they grow and grow until they are huge monsters."

That's how my dad is. Deep and insightful, he tries to understand the patterns of people's lives.

"While you were still in the hospital, Marie Roberts' grandfather came here." I could hear the emotion in my father's voice. "He came to tell us how sorry he was for what happened. I pitied him so much, and when I put my arm around him and told him we do not hold anything against him or his family, Mr. Welk broke down and cried. He told me he was not able to sleep for many nights after it happened."

I could hear Benuel stir in his chair. "Rebecca Sue, did you know that Marie has visited all the families and told them she is sorry for what Mr. Roberts did? She came here while you were in the hospital. Think how hard that must have been for her."

I nodded. In my heart I knew Mr. Roberts' family was also hurting, grieving deeply for what he had done to us. Not only to us, but also to their family, and to our community.

"If this helps you, let me tell you some more." Dad cleared his throat. "The other milk truck drivers who knew him now say he was becoming more silent and withdrawn the last several weeks. He never spoke much to anyone, as we as a family know. When he would pick up our milk, he would barely say 'hi.'

"Now I am thinking we should have been friendlier. Perhaps if we would have reached out to him more, he would never have gone through such a deep depression and ended his life this way. I feel so sorry for him."

"I heard he had been planning this for a long time before he ever did it," Benuel said slowly. "I guess he did not have any close friends to talk to about his problems."

Dad shook his head. "No, not even his wife. That hurts Marie deeply, for now she regrets not having been able to reach him during his despondency. She feels terrible."

I could not help asking, "Is it true she was with a group of women praying when this all happened?"

"Yes. She had left home that morning to go pray with the other ladies from her church. Mr. Roberts took the children to the bus stop, parked his milk truck at the auction house, then went to borrow Mr. Welk's pickup truck."

Something was still bothering me. "Why, Dad, when the ladies were praying, and we girls were praying, and Teacher Leah and the women were praying, did God still let him do what he did?"

I heard someone enter the room, and even without turning my head, I knew Mom had joined us. I was pretty sure Elam was listening from the kitchen. He had been acting strange recently, hardly ever talking to me and avoiding any mention of the happening.

"Let me tell you what I believe," my father said sincerely. "I do believe God heard all the prayers that day. In fact, I know He did. What I won't pretend to know is why He let happen what did happen. We are just a small part of the plan God has for the world. We know that, in the Bible, there were many times when God allowed evil men to create havoc. Do you remember, Rebecca Sue, when the soldiers came into Bethlehem and killed all the children two and under? Remember how it says that the mothers wept and would not be comforted? Then we ask the question, 'Why does God allow these things to happen?'

"My faith in God goes much deeper than what I can comprehend with my mind. If I understood everything, I would not have to have faith. It may never become clear to me why God allowed this tragedy, but one thing I do know—God has a plan for all of us."

The clock ticked steadily on into the evening. No one said anything for a while.

Then Elam's voice came from the kitchen doorway.

"Something as evil as taking away Sadie Mae and the girls, wounding the others, and turning every day into a sharp reminder to Miriam's family—it seems like an awfully strange way for God to teach us a lesson." I could hear the struggle in my brother's voice and was reminded again that I was not the only one trying to cope with what had happened.

"I hate to see Mr. Welk's truck going down the road, even though I know Mr. Roberts just borrowed it for that day," Elam said passionately. "It always reminds me . . ."

"Son," Dad broke in, his voice choking, "pray that God would give you grace to accept what has happened. It is hard for all of us."

The silence that followed was broken by Rosie's cry. Her sad voice echoed what we were all feeling, and Mom hurried upstairs to comfort her. As Rosie's cries faded, I wished the cries in our own hearts could be quieted so easily.

"It is a choice," Dad said, breaking into our thoughts. "We can choose to forgive, or we can choose to hang on to our hurts. If we do not forgive others, we cannot expect God to forgive our sins. The preacher said it so well at Sadie Mae's funeral."

"Some days I think I have forgiven," Elam said, his young voice husky, "but then the next day, or when I see something that belonged to Sadie Mae, like Roxie, I get bitter feelings all over again. I just wish I could forgive, then let it all be over with."

"For me," Benuel said, "I sorrow most of all for Mr. Roberts' soul. I think of the terrible place where he is now."

The lamp behind Dad's head shone around him, making a kind of halo. I am sure he did not realize it, but for me right then, his faith in spite of all the questions was about the only stable and secure thing in my life. I longed for that kind of trust.

I walked beside my mother into the hospital. Once more I was making a trip to the doctor for another checkup. Abigail, my favorite nurse, was there, and I smiled at her as she greeted me.

"There's my Rebecca Sue! My, how well you look!" She took my temperature and felt my pulse, chatting cheerily all the time. "I guess you'll soon return to school. That will be an exciting time, won't it?"

I nodded. "Yes, I want to go back as soon as I can."

"We have all been praying for you," she said sincerely. "At our church, we have been having a special prayer time every week for all of you. I know thousands of people have been supporting you in prayer."

"Thank you very much," Mom replied. "It helps to know

how many people are thinking about our families. And the widow and her family."

"Is it true," Abigail asked, "that the Amish are visiting her and that some of the donated money is being used for her needs?"

"Yes," Mom told her. "We are trying to help her with her loss as much as we can. Our hearts go out to her in this trying time. She has her three young children to care for, and it must not be easy."

Abigail shook her head slightly, and I saw a wrinkle cross her forehead. "The forgiveness you Amish are showing is just past my understanding," she said bluntly. "I would think you would want nothing to do with that guy's family. You must think about it every time you go past her house."

"My husband says every thought we have about the happening—everything we see that reminds us of Mr. Roberts—gives us another opportunity to forgive. I am trying to follow his example." My mother's face showed the effort behind her words.

"I guess that's true," Abigail agreed after a short pause. She turned and began writing on her chart. "I've read everything in the newspapers about it, and always someone from the Amish community says something about forgiveness. It's incredible, but I guess it's a lesson to the rest of us."

The newspapers. I thought again how often they printed another article about the happening. Even though it hurt, I still tried to read everything I could about what had happened. We all did. As I read about how the community had responded to the tragedy, I felt humbled and grateful for what the police, firemen, and ambulance workers had done for us.

My mind revisited something that had occurred only several days after I had come home. It had been a day when I was feeling a lot of pain from my injuries. Mom had given me a pain pill, but the throbbing ache did not want to go away.

"Rebecca Sue, there's someone here to see you," Mom had announced from the doorway of the living room.

I looked up to see English visitors entering the room—a strong-looking man and a woman, along with two children, a boy and girl. The girl was probably the age Sadie Mae had been, the boy younger.

"Hi. My name is Art Sponski, and this is my wife Judy," the man said pleasantly, looking intently at me. "And these are our children. Brian is four and Brittany is nine."

Dad had joined us. "Mr. Sponski is a policeman who helped at the schoolhouse. He wanted to come and see us . . . to see you."

"We brought some flowers for you," Mrs. Sponski spoke up

kindly, handing me a beautiful bouquet of miniature roses.

"Thank you," I managed to say as I held them up to my face.

"And I made a card for you." Brittany handed me a card with a hand-colored picture of a horse and buggy on the front.

I smiled at her as she handed it to me. "Thank you," I said once again.

"I brought this for you!" Brian held out a box. "It's candy!" he said, his eyes sparkling.

Everyone laughed, and Mom invited them to sit down.

"Rebecca Sue," Dad said, "Mr. Sponski thinks he may be the one who carried you out of the schoolhouse. He wanted to come see how you are."

I looked at his strong, kind face—and was suddenly back in the schoolhouse, feeling the strong arms of an officer taking me outside, away from the horror all around us.

"Yes," I said, "I remember. I remember you." Speaking directly to him, I added, "Thank you. Thank you for what you did for me that day."

Tears began to roll down his cheeks. "You are welcome," he said when he could speak again. "I am so glad I was able to help you. Over and over I have seen your face in my dreams. I am so thankful that you are recovering."

Mrs. Sponski had edged closer, placing her hand on her husband's shoulder. "It means a lot to my husband to be able to connect with someone from that day. We offer our sympathy and prayers."

"We are extremely grateful to every one of the officers for what they did that day," Dad said, his voice shaky. "We can never thank you enough."

"The entire community worked together in such a special way," Mrs. Sponski continued. "It was overwhelming at first to see all the people who came to help. When I think of all the food and supplies the local stores and restaurants donated, I am just grateful that we live in such a wonderful community."

"That day, and in the days that followed, we were all drawn together as one," Mr. Sponski said. "There were no differences between us. It did not matter who was Amish or non-Amish. We were all one, trying to pull ourselves together."

"I think of that over and over again," Dad agreed. "There were so many willing hands to help, whether it was to take us to the hospital, or just to plan the day. That is at least one good thing that has come out of all this."

After the Sponskis left, I lay a long time thinking about how kind everyone was. The policemen. The lady who had treated me and taken me on the ambulance. The nurses and doctors at the hospital. Our neighbors and our relatives. The blanket of love and care was for the moment a wave of warmth that shut out the cold of what had happened.

These things had all been reported in the newspapers. Time and again I had read how other officers, emergency workers, and firemen visited us families. Our family was by no means the only one feeling this generous outpouring of love and support. We were all wonderfully cared for.

And as I read about the donations, I could not grasp the amount of money that had come streaming in to help us. It had increased steadily until millions of dollars were in the fund to pay for hospital bills, funeral expenses, and anything else that needed to be paid. Building materials for the new schoolhouse had been pledged by the building supply stores in the area. "As much as we need," Benuel had said one evening. "Big Jim told us today that he heard on the radio that many business owners are trying to donate whatever is needed."

"The support is truly something to be thankful to God for," Dad said. "Who would have ever imagined so many lives would be touched?"

8

The Counseling

"I know it's because God is answering the prayers of so many people." I could hear Hannah's mother talking out in the kitchen with Mom. "The doctors told us they were sure they couldn't save Catherine's arm because her shoulder was damaged so badly."

Every week the mothers of the girls in school were getting together for support and comfort. Even though we families were from three church districts, it no longer mattered. This morning the other women had come to our house to be with Mom.

Some of the little children were playing with Rosie in the living room, where I was sitting on the couch. Their merry chatter was a pleasant backdrop to the day, and I could overhear the women's conversation.

"Did the bullets hit the bones?" I heard another woman asking—I think it was Martha's mother.

Hannah's mom must have nodded, for she said, "The doctors said the bones were so shattered they made their own exit holes."

"Now you say she has some movement?" another woman's voice asked.

"Yes. Like I said, God must have touched her. Not only did she get to keep her arm, but she can now write with a pencil."

I could hear soft exclamations of glad surprise from the other women.

I had seen Catherine. One day her family had brought her over to visit with our family. Catherine and I had sat together on the couch. At first it had been difficult to know what to say. She was in the fifth grade, and somewhat quiet by nature. I remember I asked her if she had been conscious through the happening. Though she said she remembered some, she had already forgotten many things. Then we talked about going back to school and how glad we would be to see Teacher Leah. We didn't mention Sadie Mae or Hannah.

"Is Miriam still about the same?" someone asked from the kitchen.

The reply came slowly. "There are days when we think she is more responsive than other days. We took her to the hospital a few days ago, and on the way home, when the driver told her goodbye, it was as though she wanted to say something. She made noises in her throat. At first we couldn't figure out what she was trying to get across. Then someone asked her if Kenneth, the driver, was to say 'hi' to his son Glen, who used to work for us. She made another noise, but this time it was a more restful one."

"Isn't that something! So you think she is conscious, at least some of the time?"

There was a slight pause, then Miriam's mother said, "Yes. And we are so thankful to God for at least getting her to this point. When she was first home from the hospital, she would scream and scream, and there were many days and nights I thought I could barely take it."

Murmurs of sympathy met this statement. Peeking through the door, I saw Sarah, who had lost both of her daughters, move over to Miriam's mom and gently put her arm around the crying woman. I could see they were crying together, and I was sure the other moms were crying with them.

"Sometimes I think my lot is not as difficult," Martha's mother said brokenly. "You moms with injured girls have to face the problems every day. Our family misses Martha very much, but we do not have to see her suffer."

"Then there are others who have both lost someone and have an injured one." I recognized Lydia's mom's voice. She was still nursing her own daughter back to health.

"I think the one who suffers the most is Marie, Mr. Roberts' wife," Hannah's mom said slowly. "Whenever I begin to feel sorry for myself, I have to remember her. I often wonder how I could survive in her situation."

"I have to agree," another mom answered softly, "although there are many times I still struggle with why all this happened, and I continually have to ask God to fill my heart with forgiveness."

As the conversation flowed around the table, I was lost in my own thoughts. Once again, I thought of our loss. My sister Sadie Mae was gone. My best friend Hannah was gone. Dear little Martha was gone. The two sisters, Ruth and Susan, were gone. Miriam was helpless and could not speak. Lydia, Catherine, Joanna, and I were all in different stages of recovery. Of the eleven girls in our school, only Leona, the one who had slipped out, was not injured.

I thought about the boys. I had seen some of them at Sadie Mae's funeral, but not all, for some were brothers to the other girls who had died and were attending their funerals. My mind just whirled whenever I thought of all that had happened the week of October 2.

I looked at the little children playing with the wooden blocks. Some of them had lost a sister. Every one of them was in a family that had suffered some kind of loss or tragedy.

Then I thought back to the evening the police officer and his family had come to visit. I remembered the pain on Art Sponski's face and thought of all the other police officers who had been involved.

"He refused to accept that Sadie Mae was dead," Benuel had told us one evening about another police officer. "He insisted the medic dispatch her to the hospital."

Now I wondered what that policeman was doing. Was he feeling the same hard knot inside him, growing bigger all the time? And the emergency workers. I knew they had gone through extremely stressful times afterward as well. Stories trickled back to us through the newspapers, neighbors, and people in church.

The community was grieving. It was not uncommon, Benuel told us, to see people standing on the street corners of our little town, talking. He could see the people had been crying.

We Amish children normally attend funerals with our parents, even before we're old enough to comprehend what is happening. By the time we enter school, it's a part of our lives. Elderly aunts, uncles, cousins, and grandparents die, and though we are saddened by the loss to the family, we know it is all part of God's plan.

I know these things, but the pain inside does not go away.

"She has helped me so much," Martha's mom was saying, directing my attention to the kitchen once more. "I didn't realize how important it is for me to talk about my feelings."

There was a murmur of voices as the women discussed their own meetings with counselors.

". . . I didn't realize how much our boys were going through. One evening after dark they cried when we wanted them to go get milk from Sam's. They had done it many times before, and now, all at once, they were scared. We realized then that they were frightened because of what happened, so I went with them."

". . . just because our boys weren't talking much did not mean they weren't struggling with their feelings."

". . . how difficult it was for us to sit together and tell the children we would try to answer any questions they had . . ."

"The teacher from the Crossroads School said she couldn't understand why one of her third-grade girls did not want to go to the blackboard to do her lessons like usual. Then she remembered the girl is Miriam's cousin and realized that she's afraid to turn her back to the school door."

I strained to hear what Mom was saying, but I could not hear her voice.

After some more talk, there was a rattle of teacups as the women got up, collected their children, and said their goodbyes.

My feet were stuck. I tried to move them, but could not. Something was wrapped around my ankles. Terror gripped me and I tried to yell. I could not.

There was the man again. I knew it was Mr. Roberts. Again I tried to yell, but nothing came out of my gasping mouth.

Mercifully, I awoke from my nightmare. I was lying stiff in bed. I sat up quickly, my mouth open, gasping for air. In spite of my efforts to keep back my sobs, they broke out, and I must have cried out loud in my fear.

As I returned to reality, I tried to control myself. Rosie moved restlessly in her sleep beside me. Outside in the hall I heard soft footsteps, then the door opened. "Rebecca Sue!"

It was Elam. He must have heard me, but I couldn't respond. I just gave a dry sob that tore at my chest. I heard his quick footsteps running downstairs. Soon the door opened again, and Mom was beside my bed. I was still sitting up, and when

Mom asked, "Rebecca Sue, what's wrong?" I just shivered all over.

"You are all right," she told me, trying to calm me with her words. But something in her own voice echoed my fear.

"Come downstairs," she whispered. "Rosie might wake up."

I was glad to move. Glad to get away from the scene of the terrible nightmare. When we passed the boys' bedroom door, I was aware that Elam was standing inside, listening to what was happening.

As we sat on the couch, Mom kept rubbing my arm. I couldn't stop shaking. I felt chills chase themselves all over me in spite of the thick blanket Mom put around me. Soon Dad was on the other side, and, snuggled between my parents, I finally stopped shaking.

"Rebecca Sue," Dad asked softly, "were you having a bad dream?"

I nodded, and found I could manage a quiet, "Yes."

"Was it . . . was it about the happening?"

I nodded and tried to explain. "My feet were tied. I wanted to move . . . to get loose in the worst way. Then I saw him coming toward me. Then I woke up, screaming."

Mom got up and went to the kitchen. Dad just sat beside me, saying nothing. I knew he was praying quietly.

After a while, Mom returned from the kitchen. Silently, she handed me a drink of water.

The lamp she had lit cast its comforting glow on the table by the window, pushing back the darkness of the night. The regular tick, tick of the clock was interrupted as the chimes rang three times.

That's when I began sleeping downstairs again.

"What were some of your sister's favorite things?"

The kind Mennonite lady who came to our house the next day visited pleasantly with my parents and me in the living room. She prayed with us, and her manner was so gentle and kind, I was immediately drawn to her. Even though at first we talked about other things, we eventually began talking about the happening. Then she left her seat on the rocking chair and sat on the sofa with me. She began asking about my days in school, and I found it easy to answer her questions.

Then she started asking me about Sadie Mae. And about Hannah.

The pain came back again, sharp and keen. I drew a deep breath. I found myself allowing my mind to go back to the days before. Suddenly I saw that picture of Sadie Mae running across the lawn with her puppy.

"Roxie," I said softly. "She loved Roxie, our puppy."

"Do you still have her?" Shirley asked, lifting one eyebrow and looking at me with a smile.

I nodded. I had not seen much of Roxie since I had come home. "I think so. I hear her barking sometimes."

"What else did your sister enjoy?"

I tried to think. It was painful to open up that part of my memory. "Flowers. She liked to help our neighbor, Mrs. Dabney, with her flower beds."

"I think your sister was a lively, energetic girl, right?"

I only nodded my head. I wanted to say, "She is," but I remembered I could not say that. I nodded again.

"Those times are more precious to you now than ever before, right? I know you must hurt very deeply to have lost her."

Her words were so kind, so gentle. I tried to push away the growing lump in my throat, but this time I couldn't. I began to cry with great heaving sobs. Even now, I cry when I remember. Now I can cry without the stabbing pain, but then there was such a tearing pain inside that I could not stop.

With her arm around me, Shirley kept patting me and whispering, "It's okay to cry, dear. Let it all out."

I was dimly aware that Mom and Dad were crying too.

It was then that I found out how healing tears can be.

Yes, I had cried before, especially at night. I had cried tears that had bound me all up inside. This time it was different. Something opened up within me that day that I had not realized I had been holding back. When, minutes later, my sobbing had almost stopped, I think the first thing I realized was that the weight inside me was gone. I heaved a sigh of relief—a great, huge, shaky sigh.

Shirley smiled down at me through her own tears. I saw Mom's face, and I could see the relief in her eyes. Dad was looking down at his hands on his lap, but then looked squarely at me and smiled.

"Is it okay to bring the puppy, Roxie, inside for a little while?" Shirley asked, looking at Mom.

"Oh, yes," Mom said quickly. "We used to let her inside before . . . when Sadie Mae was still alive. But I thought it might be easier on all of us not to be reminded."

Dad had already left and was soon back with Roxie.

"She's hardly a puppy anymore," Shirley laughed as frisky little Roxie began jumping up and down in excitement.

"Roxie!" I laughed through my tears, and she jumped up and licked my face.

Shirley came a number of times after that, and we talked about many things. She helped me face my fears, and we talked about the importance of letting our feelings out. "God made us with emotions, and hurt people have to learn that it is all right to cry, and also to be happy and laugh again. This is the way God made us. We should not feel guilty about enjoying life again, even after a tragedy."

There were times when our entire family sat together and talked. We played games in the evenings as the days grew shorter and the cold weather arrived. But now the cold stayed outside where it belonged.

9

The Teacher

Once I learned it was all right to talk about my feelings and how I missed my sister and my friends, I ventured out of my own world and started wondering how other people were coping. So when Teacher Leah and her family stopped by to visit one evening, I welcomed the opportunity to hear what they had to share.

"The minute I heard what was happening, I rushed over to the school with the driver who brought the news," Corner Sam said. "I was distraught. I thought my wife and daughters and Lizzie and Sylvia and the grandchildren were all inside—all the girls except for Katie."

Their youngest daughter, Katie, attends Wolf Rock Amish School, within sight of our school. She is my age.

"When we reached the crossroads, the police were clearing everyone out to make way for the ambulances. I thought I just had to get in there to see what was going on. Some men had to hold me back from running down the road." He shook his head at the memory.

"We were already out by then," his wife, Mary, reminded him. "But of course you didn't know that."

"No," Corner Sam continued. "All I could do was stand there and shake. And pray."

Benuel spoke up. "Were a lot of other people there already? I mean, even before the shooting started?"

"I know Jacob and his son-in-law Enos both raced down across the meadow to the school after Leah ran up and told them to call 9-1-1. Enos told me later that he walked right up to a window and tried to peer inside, but the shades were drawn. Jacob told me they tried to hide behind the maple tree, then behind the outhouses."

"What about the boys?" Elam wanted to know. "Were they already at the farm?"

Nodding, Corner Sam answered, "Yes. They had been hiding behind the boys' outhouse, but when the women who had left the schoolhouse earlier saw them there, they motioned to them to follow, and they all ran up to the farm."

"We heard the police sirens from our school," Katie spoke up. "We all ran outside and stood on the fence looking down at the Nickel Mines School. Someone drove up and told us a man with a gun was inside."

It felt strange to be hearing what had happened outside our school. I looked at my friend for a long time. She turned to me and said, "Our teacher led us inside and we knelt beside our desks and prayed for you."

I reached out and took her hand. "Thank you," I whispered.

"We heard the policeman talking to Mr. Roberts through the loudspeaker," Katie continued. "We were all so scared. I knew my mom and the others had gone to visit. I could barely stop shaking."

Teacher Leah took up the story. "Once I told Enos to call 9-1-1, I didn't know what to do. I joined the others who were standing out beside the barn, and we watched as all the police cars came streaming in. Then I saw the crowd gathering by the crossroads. I just could not think what I should be doing. When Lizzie and Sylvia and Malinda arrived with the children, I suddenly realized that Leona was with them. 'I just ran out,' she told me when I was so amazed to see her."

"We all just walked around in a daze," Mary remembered. "More and more people kept coming. Amish, English, just everybody. All had questions, but hardly anyone had answers. We told them what we knew, but of course no one had any clue how bad it was."

"Then the helicopters started flying in," Corner Sam said. "The sky was full of whirling blades and pulsing motors. Ambulances, fire trucks, cars, and trucks jammed the roads. It looked like a war zone."

"I think the hardest part was not knowing what was happening inside," Dad said slowly. "By the time we arrived, all we could do was join the crowd of people across the road and watch . . . and wait."

Mom dabbed at her eyes with her handkerchief. "I couldn't stand it, so I went up to the farm. I remember seeing one of the mothers crying on a neighbor lady's shoulder. Later I learned that her husband was still at work, and she felt so alone."

"I know just having so many friends there was a great comfort, even if no one knew what to do or say," Mary said, wiping her own eyes. "Now I look back and realize how wonderful it is to be a part of a caring, loving community."

"Not only the Amish," Dad agreed. "That day, it did not matter if someone was Amish, Mennonite, or English. We were all one."

Corner Sam nodded, his gray beard moving up and down.

"That's the way it should be. Everyone working together to help."

I thought of our neighbors, the Dabneys, and how they had been so kind in so many ways. They had used their minivan to haul people all over the place. Every time I needed to go to the hospital for treatments, they took us, if they could, spending long hours on the road and even more hours just waiting.

"So many have helped," Corner Sam spoke up again. "We will never know how many people worked long and hard— without pay, too."

"I hope the men handling the funds will pay as many of those volunteers as they can," Dad said.

"Yes," Corner Sam agreed, "they are trying to pay those who helped. Some only take a little for gas, and many refuse to take anything. Such generosity is amazing."

"You know how we are used to helping families during a viewing and the days before a funeral?" Elam spoke up. "We had so many offers to help here at our farm, and it was not only the Amish. Everyone wanted to help in some way."

"Leah," Mom looked at my teacher, "how are you coping?"

"Oh, I have my times," Leah admitted honestly. "But my favorite times, and the most healing, are when I'm teaching school. Every time another one of my girls comes back to school, it makes my days much brighter." She smiled at me, and I smiled back.

"I was so grateful for the support of my friends. When the police officer came to the farm and asked me if I would go down to the schoolyard to identify the girls, I needed someone to go with me. My friend Anna volunteered to go, and I can tell you, that was such a comfort. By the time we got there, the girls were gone, but the police had taken pictures and wanted me to use them to identify the girls. All the time I was down there, I could sense love and concern from Anna, and from the police officers. As difficult as it was, it was made bearable by those who cared."

"Weekends are the hardest for her," her mom explained. "I can tell. I'm a mother, you know." She laughed a little.

"That's when she plans things to do for others," Corner Sam said. "I know she's planning to go Christmas caroling soon. I saw her list of songs to practice."

"But I don't suffer like your family does, or like many of the others who lost daughters or have to deal with the hurt ones," Leah said. "I often think of you others who go through much more than I do."

"You suffer enough," Mary said, almost sharply. "You have to deal with what others are saying about you running out."

"I still sometimes think . . ." Leah started to speak, but her dad cut her off.

"None of that. You did not know what was going to happen. You left your students in the care of your mother and risked disobeying the gunman in order to run for help. Your responsibility was, and is, your school children, and when you went for help, that was the right thing to do."

Benuel spoke up. "After a tragedy, there are always people who ask why someone did things a certain way or why someone didn't do something differently. I think that's unnecessary. None of us know what we would do in a crisis."

Heads nodded in agreement.

"In spite of the terrible things that happened," Corner Sam said, "there are still so many things to be thankful for. I know God was looking after all of us during those terribly stressful times. After I quieted down, I could just feel that, whatever was going on in the schoolhouse, God was in control. I am so thankful now for all the teaching I've had to trust in God."

Once again there was a murmur of assent. I felt safe in my own knowledge that, like David the Psalmist wrote, "My help cometh from the Lord." That was a verse I had learned in our memory class at school. More than once since the happening, I have had verses from the Bible come to me just when I need them.

"I guess there are plenty of funds for the new school," Elam offered. "I heard that many building supply businesses have offered materials to build the school."

"Several million dollars came in," Corner Sam said. "Thousands of letters came to the firehouse, and over half of the letters had money inside. It's unbelievable how many people have responded so generously to our needs."

"Why did the mail go to the firehouse?" I wondered.

Corner Sam turned to look at me. Shaking his head slightly, he answered, "I guess you were in the hospital too long to see what a crowded, busy place the firehouse was. You see, Rebecca Sue, so much mail came from all over the United States, and even from foreign countries, that our local post office couldn't handle it all. So the mail was sent to the firehouse, and as many as five volunteers at a time spent hours sorting it all."

Mom nodded. "We still haven't opened all our mail. After opening hundreds of envelopes, it gets tiring, but we sure do appreciate that so many people are thinking about us. People have been extremely generous, both with sympathy and with doing all they can to help, with money or otherwise."

Dad nodded. "Our hospital has not charged us for anything. I think most of Rebecca Sue's bills have been canceled. It's amazing how people have responded more than adequately to meet our needs."

"It's good that the elders appointed an accountability committee to take care of the donations," Mom said. "It's a big relief for us not to have to look after all that. Those men work hard to make sure all our financial needs are taken care of. Just handling all the donated money has taken a lot of time."

"I no longer see Mr. Welk's truck on the road," Elam spoke up. "I think that has made it easier for me to forget what happened and move on with life."

"It has helped all of us," Corner Sam said. "The committee approached Mr. Welk to see how he would feel about getting another truck so we wouldn't have to face our emotions every time we saw it on the road. He was very understanding about it."

The grownups continued to talk. Teacher Leah sat beside me on the sofa. "Rebecca Sue, don't worry about your lessons in school. I'll work with you once you return and let you begin your lessons wherever you need to start."

"Thank you," I answered gratefully. Schoolwork did not always come easily for me. Not like it had for Hannah.

"It is really hard to adjust to having the girls missing," Teacher Leah said, sensing my thoughts. "The boys talk about how strange it felt the first few days to only have Leona in school. I know they will be glad when the rest of you girls come back. Catherine is back, you know. I hope you and Lydia and Joanna can all be back soon."

"Leona . . ." I was curious. "Does she ever talk about how she got away? What made her leave? I never found out when she left. All at once she was just gone."

Teacher Leah smoothed her dress with her hand. "It is absolutely amazing sometimes how young children can deal with things. Did you know that the afternoon of the happening, she went home to bake cookies? While the rest of us were waiting in suspense, she was doing something to occupy herself."

I couldn't help but giggle. "That sounds so like her."

"Absolutely. No, in school she does not have much to say about her escape. She said once that she heard someone tell her, 'Now would be a good time to go out,' but she doesn't know who talked to her. Some people think it must have been an angel, but I guess no one knows for sure."

Angels. A warm feeling swept over me at the reminder of where Sadie Mae and the other girls were. I felt that way every time someone brought angels into the conversation.

"Once she said she wasn't obedient like the rest of you girls, since she slipped out instead of lying down like she was told to," Teacher Leah continued. "I guess that bothered her for a little bit."

Then Teacher Leah was quiet. I looked up at her.

"When I saw that you had gone to call for help," I told her

slowly, "I was so glad. I knew you would do everything you could to get help for us. It gave me something to hope for while I was down there on that floor."

"Thank you," Teacher Leah replied. "I really didn't think much about what I was doing. I just ran as fast as I could to get help."

We were both silent for a while. Mom had gone to the kitchen and returned with a plate of Christmas cookies. She passed them around.

"I hope I can go Christmas caroling with you, Teacher Leah," I said, munching on my cookie.

"Yes, I'd love that! We want to go sing for Mrs. Roberts." I could hear kindness in my teacher's voice. "I know she suffers so much. I have seen her and her three children a number of times recently, and I can see she is so sorry about what happened."

"She came here with her grandfather one evening before I returned from the hospital," I told her. "My mom said she hugged her and they cried together."

"She has visited all of the families," Teacher Leah said. "I think she is a brave woman, and we must do everything we can to support her."

"Do the boys talk about what happened?" I asked.

Teacher Leah nodded. "Yes, they do, and at first I wasn't

sure how to handle it. They began discussing the events among themselves, and although we don't talk about it as much now, hardly a day passes that we don't mention something about it."

"Was it hard to set up school in a garage?"

"Not really. The next Monday the school board took the boys and me—and Leona—back to the schoolhouse. I took our name charts and things off the walls, and the boys took the things they wanted. The schoolhouse was clean and orderly again. It was weird—as though nothing bad had ever happened there, and yet we were all aware that something dreadful had happened. We had attended the funerals, gone through the grief, suffering, and emotions of the previous week, and now here we were, back again.

"One thing that really helped was how cheerful the boys and Leona were. They went through their desks, gathering their personal things and putting them into their backpacks. At eleven o'clock, we all bowed our heads in silent prayer. Someone rang the bell, then someone else had the idea that we all should take hold of the bell rope and ring it. But the rope broke." She chuckled at the memory. "That made everyone laugh, and we all felt more cheerful."

"Teacher Leah," I wanted to know, "how do you handle all the thoughts that come to you?"

Her voice was gentle. "It is only by the grace of God,

Rebecca Sue. I tell you, it is wonderful to feel His peace in my heart. When I am troubled, I pray. When I can't sleep, I pray. At the farm, when I did not know what all was happening down at the schoolhouse, I saw my friend Anna crossing the yard to meet me. We hugged and cried together. Then we walked around the corner of the shop and she prayed with me. I guess I never knew how much strength a person can receive from prayer."

With a gentle sigh, Teacher Leah continued. "It was such a relief once the schoolhouse was torn down. I hated to see it all boarded up, with the yellow tape surrounding the schoolyard. Some went to watch them tear it down, but I stayed away. I was busy getting the garage set up."

"Did you want them to tear down the schoolhouse?" I asked softly.

Teacher Leah did not respond immediately. Then, looking at me kindly, she said, "At first I did not think about it that much. But after I heard our school board and the parents talk about it, I could see the wisdom in their decision. We feel it is easier to go on with our lives if the schoolhouse is gone. Does that make sense?"

I nodded. I was beginning to understand.

"Also, many curious people were driving past just to look at the schoolhouse. Some even wanted to build some kind of museum or something across the road. We didn't want that. We were afraid the stream of visitors would last much longer if there was actually something to look at."

I nodded again. "Is that why the schoolhouse was torn down early in the morning, before dawn?"

"Yes. Even so, there were reporters there, taking pictures."

"It's hard for me to understand why people are so interested in what happened."

Teacher Leah smiled. "I used to wonder about that too. But then I thought about how I react when something happens in another community. I guess we're no different."

That was true. I had listened to the grownups' conversations. Whenever something exciting or unusual happened, we could not get over talking about it.

Teacher Leah continued. "The firemen and the policemen were there to make sure no one grabbed anything for souvenirs. The trucks were covered with tarps and the stuff was taken to the landfill. By midmorning even the white board fence was gone, and the place was turned back into a part of the meadow."

"But they're building us a new schoolhouse, right?" I wanted to hear it from my teacher.

Teacher Leah nodded. "Although I don't mind having

school in the garage. It has really worked out well."

"I can't wait to come back," I told her. "I really miss school, and even though it won't be the same, I still want to come back."

Teacher Leah gave me a hug as her family got ready to leave.

That evening I felt that life could go on. Like Shirley had said, it was all right to grieve and miss those who had died, and it was also all right to enjoy each other again, even in the midst of our loss. Plus, I was so grateful that my nightmares had not returned. At times I still had troubling dreams, but not as frequently. And that terrible weight inside my chest was gone.

10

The Helpers

"I so wanted to meet you again," Lisa McNight said warmly. "For a long time, I did not know which of you girls I helped."

I smiled at the friendly woman who had come to our farm that evening. "I'm glad to meet you too," I answered shyly.

"And we can never thank you enough for what you did for our daughter that day," Mom said gratefully. Dad nodded in agreement.

"We did what we were trained to do," Lisa said, then added, "but we'd never had such a situation before." Then she stopped speaking and looked at me.

"It's all right," Dad assured her, interpreting the look. "Rebecca Sue is comfortable talking about it."

"I didn't want to cause any further trauma," Lisa said. "We had debriefings as emergency responders, and it has really helped us to talk about what happened."

"It has been very healing for us as a family also," Mom's voice betrayed deep feeling. "I don't know how we could have coped without having people to talk with. For a long time I tried to push everything out of my mind, but it didn't work. I had bad dreams, and even though I didn't realize it, a pressure was building up inside me that was hard to live with."

"I know what you mean," Lisa agreed, tears forming in her own eyes.

"Truly God has been good to all of us during this time," Dad said after a silence had filled our living room. "I know many people have been praying. We have all felt that."

Lisa nodded. "To hear you say that after you have lost one daughter and had another one injured is healing for my heart. Sometimes, when I get so angry at what happened, I have to deliberately turn my thoughts away from all this and see how kind you people have been through it all."

"It is because of what God has done in our lives," Dad repeated. "We believe that God did not want this to happen, but He allowed it. His ways are higher than our ways, and we are not asked to understand, but to believe and trust in Him when we don't understand." His words were spoken simply, without pride, and from his heart. I know this because I know my father. This is how he lives his faith.

"I know one thing," Lisa said. "The forgiveness your people have shown will be a shining example all over the world."

Dad nodded. "We pray that people may see not what we are doing, but what God is doing. We are but weak humans who need power from God to forgive."

He paused, then continued. "It has been said before, but we need to tell ourselves often, that forgiveness is a choice. We can choose to forgive, or we can choose to hang on to bitterness and anger and live miserable lives. That is definitely not what God wants for His children."

Just then Rosie tottered in from the kitchen. Lisa turned to her. "Hi! What is your name?"

Rosie was getting used to having lots of visitors at our house, but she was still shy with people who did not speak Pennsylvania German. So she just grinned.

"This is Rosie," Mom answered for her. "She's our little sunshine."

"I'm sure," Lisa smiled. "What a comfort for you to have a little one to love and cuddle after all you have gone through."

"Oh, yes," Mom nodded. "There were many evenings I

rocked Rosie to sleep after the happening, not because she needed it, but because I needed it. Long after she was asleep, I just held her on into the night, feeling her warm little body pressing my lap, thankful that God has spared us our baby."

Then, looking at me, Mom said softly, "And I know I don't say it often enough, but I am also so thankful that God has spared Rebecca Sue. I now realize more than ever that our children are gifts from God. Every one He allows us to have and to raise is a precious gift. I hope I never take any of my children for granted again."

Then I felt something I had wondered if I would ever feel again. A feeling of family flooded my heart, so strong and comforting I cannot describe it. I looked around and saw my family—Dad, so wise and faithful; Mom, caring and loving; Benuel, quiet and thoughtful; Elam, full of life, struggling over and over to forgive, yet finding the grace to do it; and our little Rosie, the sunshine of all our lives. And me—someone God had seen fit to save from death.

And Sadie Mae—someone God had seen fit to gather to Himself.

It was pleasant now to think of Sadie Mae. I could picture her in heaven, running among the white clouds with the little angels, free from pain and worry and singing songs at the top of her lungs.

I didn't realize I was crying until Dad asked, "Rebecca Sue, are you all right?"

His gentle voice brought me back to reality. I nodded. "I was just thinking about how happy Sadie Mae and my classmates are up in heaven, running around with the angels and singing . . . Wait, not running! Flying! Sadie Mae must just love flying!"

We laughed together.

In my imagination, I saw my younger sister all dressed in white and flapping silver wings, singing as she hovered close to the golden throne where God sat, smiling at all of them.

"What a wonderful thing to think about!" Lisa said. "I, too, am going to think about that whenever I think about the happening."

"Feel free to come anytime," Mom told Lisa as she said goodbye. "You are always welcome."

"I will come back," Lisa promised. Turning to me, she said, "Goodbye, Rebecca Sue. Always keep your faith in God."

"The firehouse was simply crawling with people," Elam told me one Sunday. "Hundreds and hundreds of them." We were looking at the pictures in the newspapers and reading the articles about how the roads had been blocked during the days of the funerals.

"What were they doing?" I asked. "Why would there be so many people there?"

"I don't know what all of them were doing," Elam told me. "But I know officials were there to answer questions for the news media, and investigators were writing down everything that had happened. There were also people making sure the roads were cleared for the funeral processions. The firemen, the police, and the county officials all needed a place to do their jobs, so the firehouse became the center of activity. The stores and restaurants donated food, and that had to be stored somewhere also."

"People ate there?" It seemed a strange scene in my mind.

"Oh, yes. Hundreds. Amish ladies and English ladies worked all day, preparing food. Every time I went there, someone was working in the kitchen."

We stared at the pictures, then Elam said, "You know, I feel differently about the police after all this. Before, I was always kind of scared of them. I thought of them coming after us if we had done something wrong and of the possibility of being arrested. But now I see them as men who really are good. They were so helpful during that time. They looked out for us and offered whatever help they could. If it would not have been for them, I wonder if we could even have had a normal funeral for Sadie Mae. They just took control and kept people back as much as they could."

For me, it was too dizzying to imagine. "I guess I will never understand," I said, "why all these people showed up and why there was such a commotion."

"A lot of people don't understand," Benuel said from his seat across the room. He had been reading and, I now realized, listening to our conversation. "And I know it's difficult for us sometimes, but this is not just our pain. Something inside people is deeply touched by tragic happenings—especially if children are involved, because they are so innocent and helpless."

"That's a long speech, coming from you," Elam teased, then he sobered. "But I think you may be closer to the truth than those of us who become upset about all the publicity."

Benuel continued. "We have to think of the ones who heard the news and want to do something about it—something to show their love and concern. It's healing for them to be able to help in some small way."

I thought of the hundreds of cards and letters we had received. "Like sending cards," I said.

"Absolutely," Elam replied. "I wonder when we will stop getting mail. The letters just keep coming."

"All written by people who care," Benuel said with a smile.

"I guess you're almost ready to go back to school," Mommi said cheerfully. I had slipped over to my grandparents' house to spend an evening with them.

"Oh, yes! I can hardly wait!"

"Over and over I have thanked God that you are healing so well." Dawdi's wrinkled face beamed at me. "Truly, miracles have happened."

At first I hadn't realized how rapidly my injuries were healing. Only when the doctors, nurses, and my relatives would exclaim about how quickly I was recovering would I realize that, somehow, God was doing something wonderful for me. I am truly grateful, but I guess I just expected that from God.

Now I looked at my grandparents. They were so special to me. Mommi always liked it when we grandchildren came over to spend evenings with them. Dawdi often gave us little treats from his pockets. Spending time with my Dad's parents was such a special part of my life. I could not imagine it any other way. Yet I knew that, someday, they would grow older and pass away. It was all a part of life.

I was too little to remember when my mother's mom had

died. But I was ten when we attended the funeral of Ammon Dawdi, as we called Mom's father. So it was always in my mind that someday Mommi and Dawdi would also pass away.

"What are you thinking about?" Mommi asked kindly.

"Oh, just about life. And death."

For a moment, we sat in the circle of light that shone steadily from the kerosene lamp.

"Only one life, 'twill soon be past. Only what's done for Christ will last." Dawdi's voice quavered as he repeated the familiar poem. It must be his favorite saying. He has quoted it for as long as I can remember.

"We brought you some early Christmas presents!" a cheery voice announced from the front door. "Merry Christmas!"

"Come in! Come in!" Mom's face beamed her welcome.

A gust of frigid air blew into the kitchen, and I could feel the draft in the living room. I got up to see who it was.

"Rebecca Sue! See who's here!" Mom called.

It was the policeman, Art Sponski, and his family. "Hi, Rebecca!" Mrs. Sponski called out in greeting. Her face was beaming. "On your feet! How wonderful!"

Mr. Sponski strode over and shook my hand. "This is one of the most wonderful Christmas presents I could ever get, to see you up on your feet again." His voice choked slightly.

"We brought your family some Christmas presents," Mrs. Sponski smiled. "Brittany and Brian have been helping us choose and wrap each present."

Rosie, attracted by the bright wrapping paper, could not resist staring longingly at the boxes.

"I see someone is getting excited about Christmas," Mrs. Sponski laughed.

"Open it," Brittany urged, handing Rosie a package.

"Is it okay?" Mrs. Sponski looked at Mom.

"That's fine," Mom answered. "In fact, I think it would be a good idea for everyone to open their presents while Officer Sponski's family is here."

"Oh, please call us Art and Judy," Judy insisted. "It makes us more like family."

That was it! Like family!

I pondered that as we sat together that evening, happily opening our presents. When Mom made tea and brought out Christmas cookies, we really were like family. Rosie soon lost her shyness and pushed the baby carriage around the living room. Brian helped by turning the carriage whenever she got too close to furniture or the wall.

"I bought this especially for you," Brittany said as she handed me a package. "To help you remember your sister."

As I unwrapped the paper, I saw a lovely picture book about angels. I breathed a quiet "thank you" as I opened the book and looked through Bible verses and poems about angels on page after page. "This is beautiful! Look, Mom!"

Then Mom told the Sponskis how I had imagined Sadie Mae and the others flying around in heaven, all dressed in white. "We know Sadie Mae must enjoy her wings, for here on earth, she could hardly ever run fast enough to suit herself."

"What a beautiful thought," Judy said, looking at me with tears in her eyes. "I am sure God directed Brittany to choose that book about angels for you."

"Angels in heaven," Mr. Sponski pondered slowly. "And some angels left on earth to cheer us meanwhile."

A silence fell over our little group. But it was a comfortable silence. A silence of healing.

As always, Mr. Sponski—Art, as he wanted us to call him—shook hands with me before he left. "I know you will have a wonderful Christmas," he said. Then he shook hands with the rest of the family.

"Thank you again," Dad said. Their hands remained linked together. "We will never know all that you and the other officers have done for us. Not only for our family, but for all the families and the entire community. We will always be grateful to God for you and your comrades."

Art just nodded his head. He could not speak.

"We thank you for letting us be your friends," Judy chimed in, speaking for her husband. "This has been so healing for Art. Those first days were extremely tough for him, and after we visited you the first time, I saw my husband begin the healing process. You have helped tremendously!"

Then, with a chorus of Christmas greetings and goodbyes, they left, taking with them a gift from Mom—a paper bag with "enough cookies for us and all our relatives," as Art laughingly remarked.

11

Back to School

I was so excited about returning to school. But for some reason, as the time approached, the thought would sometimes strike me with panic. How would I cope with the loss of my sister and my friends? Could I really face going back to school after the happening? So it was with mixed feelings that I woke up that morning in early December and got ready for school.

"Welcome! Do you need any help with those steps?" Staci, our driver, asked as I got into the van.

"Thank you, but I can manage," I replied. I still had to be careful with my injuries, but every day I could move around better.

"Hi, Rebecca Sue!" The children in the van welcomed me. "We're glad to have you back."

Staci picked up the scholars every morning. In the evening, either she or someone else took everyone home again. There were several reasons for this. First, we girls who were injured needed transportation anyway, and second, there were still many reporters around trying to get stories about what had happened. So it had been arranged that we would ride to school.

"Sit with me," Catherine invited. She scooted over, making room for me beside her. She was all bundled up in her scarf and coat.

"How does it feel to be back in school?" I asked. "I mean, is it different . . ." My voice trailed off.

"It is very different," Catherine said simply. "Every day something reminds us of those who are missing. Yet it is becoming more normal again. A new normal." She smiled slightly.

We reached the crossroads in Nickel Mines. The big brown auction barn crowded the road, and I saw the red soft drink machine. Just ahead on the right was where our old schoolhouse used to stand. Now it was only an open meadow, though the maple trees still stood. The fence around the schoolyard was gone, the outhouses were gone, and the white wooden fence across the front had been replaced with regular wire fencing.

The chatter inside the van helped keep my thoughts from the happening. "We have a lot of fun playing peek-around-the-corner where we are now," one of the boys told me. "There are so many things to hide behind."

Then we were there. Stepping through the side door, I was amazed at how familiar Teacher Leah had made this temporary school.

At the long wall in the back, the blackboards were filled with the day's assignments. The charts listing the parts of speech were on a side wall—the same charts from the old school. The "Visitors Brighten Our Days" sign was there, as were the ABC cards for the first graders and the cursive letter cards for the rest of us. Cheerful snow scenes were arranged on the other side wall, and I saw several paper snowflakes on the garage door windows, reminding us of the winter season.

"I'm so glad you're back," Teacher Leah welcomed me warmly. "I thank God for every one of you who is returning to health."

Just for a moment, I felt tears sting my eyelids. But they were not bitter tears—just a feeling of longing for what had been, and also for what lay ahead.

Teacher Leah smiled her understanding and said, "I put your desk right over here. Let me know if you need anything."

". . . Thy rod and thy staff, they comfort me. Thou preparest a table before me in the presence of mine enemies. My cup runneth over. Surely, goodness and mercy shall follow me all the days of my life and I shall dwell in the house of the Lord forever." The familiar words from Psalm 23 washed over me as Teacher Leah read the morning Bible passage.

It was so true! Goodness and mercy did follow me! I reflected on all the wonderful things God had done for me. In spite of losing my sister and my friends, I could still rejoice!

"The house of the Lord is not a literal place here on earth," Teacher Leah reflected as she closed her Bible. "It is a place inside of us. A place of peace and rest."

Yes! I sensed that. Submitting to God's will made that place inside of us a house for the Lord! And with Him living there, things were peaceful. That was how it was with me. That place in me—the place where the weight had been . . . it was *ruich* (restful).

"Rebecca Sue, do you have a song you would like to sing this morning?" Teacher Leah's gentle voice brought me back from my thoughts.

"I Feel Like Traveling On," I replied without hesitation. It just came right out.

Teacher Leah gave me a meaningful look, then began singing the familiar song.

My heavenly home is bright and fair,
I feel like traveling on . . .

Then I noticed our name charts.

Every year for the last three years, Teacher Leah had made name charts for all of us students, displaying our first and last names and our grades. All twenty-six of us. For the boys, Teacher Leah had used a silhouette of a boy on a tractor. For the girls, a silhouette of a girl in a garden with flowers.

Now, stretched above the blackboard, they were all up again. From first grade through eighth grade, the name charts, decorated cheerfully, spelled out all the names of the Nickel Mines School scholars.

I found my name chart close to the end and noticed something had been added—a rainbow! The other girls who had been hurt had rainbows on their name charts too. Five rainbows, to remind us of God's promises. He would never leave us nor forsake us. He would always love us and care for us, no matter what.

And something else had been added to the charts. Five lambs. One for each of the girls who had died.

One for my sister, Sadie Mae.

One for my best friend, Hannah.

One for little Martha.

One for Susan, and one for her sister, Ruth.

Five lambs, now with the Good Shepherd. God had taken them home to Himself in heaven, where they were waiting for us.

> *Yes, I feel like traveling on!*
> *I feel like traveling on!*

I lifted my voice and joined in with the rest of the class, singing those wonderful words. I could picture the girls in heaven singing along with us, somewhere up beyond the clouds with God, happy, contented, and free.

Once more I pictured Sadie Mae running across the green lawn at home, laughing with joy. As I watched her, the picture changed. Now she was in heavenly pastures, flying with the angels and singing with a joy she could not have imagined here on earth. Hannah was in the picture now, and little Martha, and Susan, and Ruth . . .

> *My heavenly home is bright and fair,*
> *I feel like traveling on!*

As the last note faded, I noticed Teacher Leah watching me. Her eyes were wet, and I realized there were tears on my own cheeks. I smiled to show her they were tears of joy, wishing I could share the picture in my mind with her. I wanted to tell her that the girls were all right—that we would all be all right.

The smile she returned was so tender, so full of understanding, I realized she already knew.

Epilogue

Someone would have to show you the precise spot where Nickel Mines Amish School used to be, or you would never find it. All traces of the school's foundations are gone. There is no memorial, no row of crosses, no indication that a schoolhouse ever used to stand in one corner of the farm pasture where workhorses and cows now graze. Once an informed person indicates the spot, you can see an apron of blacktop beside the county road where the driveway used to be. That is all.

Unless you notice the maple trees. They are still there, standing about forty feet tall, fenced in to keep the farm animals from harming them. Three of them. One stood on each side of the school, and a smaller one stood behind it. Now they provide shade on hot, sunny days for the cattle and horses.

The schoolyard has been seeded over and is now part of the pasture. The meadow grass has taken root and grows lush and green like the rest of the pasture, leaving no trace of what used to be there.

This unmarked spot is in keeping with how the Amish are dealing with the happening. The maple trees and the green meadow grass may symbolize more precisely than any monument how the community is handling its heartbreak.

Living trees. Slowly growing, branching out and providing places for birds to nest and raise their young. Going on, doing what they have been created to do.

Green grass. Putting down deep roots, providing food for the farm animals, and growing back again.

This corner of the pasture—this spot shaded by maple trees—is perhaps the most fitting memorial of all to the courage and resilience of the people of Nickel Mines. Let it be a living memorial for all of us.

As for the garage, it is a garage once more. On April 2, 2007, exactly six months after the happening, the teacher and her students moved into New Hope School.

Nickel Mines School

Medical helicopters wait in the pasture beside the school.

News media set up at the Nickel Mines Auction just up the road from the school. Police had taped off the road leading to the school and the farm where the families gathered. This was as close as the media were allowed to the scene.

People left notes, flowers, stuffed animals, and balloons at this makeshift memorial near the Nickel Mines crossroads just up from the school. As soon as a new pile would appear, the Amish would take the items to the firehouse to be distributed elsewhere. Though the Amish appreciated people's thoughtfulness, they did not want that kind of a memorial. People eventually started taking their gifts and donations directly to the firehouse.

TV media crews were assigned a post outside Nickel Mines where they camped for days waiting for interviews or photo opportunities to add to their newscasts.

Troopers block streets and guard the roads in preparation for one of the funeral processions. Many property owners put up tape to keep the media off their lawns and prevent people from parking. The police even got a federal order for a no fly zone over the whole area during the funerals so people could not observe or take pictures. The Nickel Mines area was guarded so that only people with passes could go in or out.

Emergency personnel headquartered at the fire department handled the logistics.

Mounted police escort one of the four funeral processions from the service to the Amish cemetery in Georgetown.

Firemen, police officers, county officials, and people from the community line the roads as the funeral procession passes, removing hats out of respect for the slain.

Media lining the road in Georgetown, anticipating a funeral procession.

The Amish began demolishing the Nickel Mines schoolhouse long before daybreak in the hopes of avoiding media attention. Nevertheless, the cameras were there. Police escorted the dump trucks to the landfill so curiosity seekers would not try to collect souvenirs. By morning, the schoolhouse was gone.

Early that same morning, the fence was replaced and the pasture seeded.

The crisis drew the community together in many ways. Firemen invited the boys from Nickel Mines School to tour the firehouse. There the Amish children enjoyed a rare opportunity to dress up in firemen's suits.

Photos courtesy of Bart Township Fire Company

About the Author

Harvey Yoder was working in his JCPenney catalog store when he first heard the news of the shooting at Nickel Mines Amish School. He, along with the rest of the world, was shocked. The rest of the day, customers kept asking, "Did you hear?" and "Do you know any of those people?"

Harvey did not know the people involved. But his mother had taught in a little schoolhouse in Lancaster County before she married, so he felt ties to the area and followed the incident with concern.

Eventually the media clamor died down, and the people of Nickel Mines were relieved to be out of the national spotlight. So Harvey's first reaction to the suggestion that he write a book on the subject was, "Why?" He wondered what purpose it could serve to dredge up memories of such a terrible tragedy and refocus attention on these peaceful people.

But a preliminary trip to the Nickel Mines area convinced Harvey that there were reasons this story should be told. Later, when he and his wife Karen moved into the community for a month-long stay, the incidents of October 2, 2006, and the weeks that followed absorbed him completely. Harvey interviewed emergency response workers, neighbors, friends, and extended family. As he saw their tears and listened to their pain, grief, and questions, he realized the community was still deeply affected by what had happened.

Harvey, too, was deeply affected. Later, as he was writing, he was often overcome with emotion and had to stop typing because he could no longer see the keyboard. He wanted to help—to be able to give some reason for the happening, some comfort to those who were suffering, some answers to the many questions.

It is his prayer that this book can help bring healing, closure, and acceptance, both to the community of Nickel Mines and to the broader community of people whose hearts were touched by the happening. And that, in all things, God would be glorified.

Harvey and Karen live near the Blue Ridge Parkway in the scenic mountains of western North Carolina. They have been married for over thirty years and have five children and four grandchildren. Though he still manages his catalog store, Harvey is devoting more and more time to his writing. He has traveled all over the world writing his twelve other books, most of which have been published by Christian Aid Ministries and are listed in the back of this book. *Not in Despair* was published by Christian Light Publications in Harrisonburg, Virginia.

Harvey enjoys hearing from readers and can be contacted by e-mail at harveyoder@juno.com or written in care of Christian Aid Ministries.

Christian Aid Ministries

Christian Aid Ministries (CAM) was founded in 1981 as a nonprofit, tax-exempt, 501(c)(3) organization. Our primary purpose is to provide a trustworthy, efficient channel for Amish, Mennonite, and other conservative Anabaptist groups and individuals to minister to physical and spiritual needs around the world.

Annually, CAM distributes fifteen to twenty million pounds of food, clothing, medicines, seeds, Bibles, *Favorite Stories from the Bible*, and other Christian literature. Most of the aid goes to needy children, orphans, and Christian families. The main purposes of giving material aid are to help and encourage God's people and to bring the Gospel to a lost and dying world.

CAM's international headquarters are in Berlin, Ohio. CAM has a 55,000 square feet distribution center in Ephrata, Pennsylvania, where food parcels are packed and other relief shipments are organized. Next to the distribution center is our meat canning facility. CAM is also associated with seven clothing centers—located in Indiana, Iowa, Illinois, Maryland, Pennsylvania, West Virginia, and Ontario, Canada—where clothing, footwear, comforters, and fabric are received, sorted, and prepared for shipment overseas.

CAM has staff, warehouses, and distribution networks in Romania, Moldova, Ukraine, Haiti, Nicaragua, and Liberia. Through our International Crisis program we also help victims of famine, war, and natural disasters throughout the world. In the USA, volunteers organized under our Disaster Response Services program help rebuild in lower income communities devastated by natural disasters such as floods, tornadoes, and hurricanes. We operate an orphanage and dairy farm in Romania, medical clinics in Haiti and Nicaragua, and hold Bible-teaching seminars in Eastern Europe and Nicaragua.

CAM's ultimate goal is to glorify God and enlarge His kingdom. ". . . whatsoever ye do, do all to the glory of God" (1 Corinthians 10:31).

CAM is controlled by a twelve-member board of directors and operated by a three-member executive committee. The organizational structure includes an audit review committee, executive council, ministerial committee, several support committees, and department managers.

Aside from management personnel and secretarial staff, volunteers do most of the work at CAM's warehouses. Each year, volunteers at our warehouses and on Disaster Response Services projects donate approximately 100,000 hours.

CAM issues an annual, audited financial statement to its entire mailing list (statements are also available upon request). Fund-raising and non-aid administrative expenses are kept as low as possible. Usually these expenses are about one percent of income, which includes cash and donated items in kind.

For more information or to sign up for CAM's monthly newsletter, please write or call:

Christian Aid Ministries
P.O. Box 360
Berlin, OH 44610
Phone: 330-893-2428
Fax: 330-893-2305

Additional Books
by Christian Aid Ministries

God Knows My Size!
by Harvey Yoder

Raised in communist Romania, Silvia Tarniceriu struggled to believe in God. But His direct answer to her earnest prayer convinced Silvia that God is real, and that He knows all about her. This book is excellent for family reading time.

251 pages $10.99

They Would Not Be Silent
by Harvey Yoder

In this book, each of the stories about Christians under communism is unique, yet one mutual thread runs throughout—They Would Not Be Silent concerning their devotion to the Lord Jesus.

231 pages $10.99

They Would Not Be Moved
by Harvey Yoder

A sequel to *They Would Not Be Silent*, this book contains more true stories about Christians who did not lose courage under the cruel hand of communism. It is our prayer that the moving stories will encourage you and help you to be stronger in your faith in the Lord Jesus Christ and more thankful for the freedoms we enjoy in our country.

208 pages $10.99

Elena—Strengthened Through Trials
by Harvey Yoder

Born into a poor Christian family in communist Romania, after harsh treatment at a state boarding school and harassment from authorities for helping in secret Bible distribution, Elena finally decides to flee her home country. Will she make it? A true story.

240 pages $10.99

Where Little Ones Cry

by Harvey Yoder

This is a story about war in Liberia. In the midst of the terror that war brings are the little children. Their stories, a few of which are captured in this book, are not of typical, carefree children. Some of these true accounts have happy endings, but sad trails lead them there. The purpose of this book is not to entertain, but to help you appreciate our blessed country more and create awareness of the pain and spiritual darkness that abound in much of Africa.

168 pages plus 16-page color picture section $10.99

Wang Ping's Sacrifice

by Harvey Yoder

The true stories in this book vividly portray the house church in China and the individuals at its heart. Read how the church—strong, flourishing, and faithful in spite of persecution—is made up of real people with real battles. Witness their heartaches and triumphs, and find your own faith strengthened and refreshed.

191 pages $10.99

A Small Price to Pay

by Harvey Yoder

Living in the Soviet Union under cruel, atheistic communism and growing up during World War II, young Mikhail Khorev saw much suffering and death. Often homeless and near starvation, he struggled to believe in God's love. This inspiring story of how Mikhail grew to be a man of God, willing to suffer prison for the God who loved him, will move you to tears and strengthen your faith. You, too, will come to realize that everything we can give to the Christ who saves us is still . . . A Small Price to Pay.

247 pages $11.99

Tears of the Rain

by Ruth Ann Stelfox

The moving story of a missionary family struggling to help some of the poorest people in the world—the men, women, and children of war-torn Liberia. Vividly descriptive and poignantly honest, this story will have you laughing on one page and crying on the next.

479 pages $13.99

Tsunami!—from a few that survived

by Harvey Yoder

Just like that, one of the greatest natural disasters in modern history approached the city of Banda Aceh, Indonesia. For most people, the cries of "Water!" reached them too late. But some survived to tell the story.

As you read the accounts in this book, you will experience, in a small degree, a few of the horrors that the people of Banda Aceh faced. Some tell their stories with sorrow and heartbreak, others with joy and hope.

168 pages $11.99

A Greater Call

by Harvey Yoder

Born into a poor family in famine-racked China, young Wei was left to die. But God had a different plan. Wei would one day answer a greater call. The cost would be enormous, but to Wei and other Chinese Christians, Jesus Christ was worth any sacrifice.

195 pages $11.99

Angels in the Night

by Pablo Yoder

Pablo's family had endured more than a dozen robberies during their first two years as missionaries in Nicaragua. But God had called them to Waslala, and they had faith that He would protect them.

In spite of the poverty and violence that surrounded them, a fledgling church was emerging, and a light, small at first but growing steadily, was piercing the darkness.

Angels in the Night continues the story begun in *Angels Over Waslala*, chronicling the trials and joys of this missionary family.

356 pages $12.99

Steps to Salvation

The Bible says that we have all "sinned and come short of the glory of God" (Romans 3:23). This means that since we have all sinned against God we need to be reconciled to Him. This is a matter of life and death, of heaven or hell (Romans 6:23; 6:16; Deuteronomy 30:19). "For God so loved the world, that he gave his only begotten Son, that whosoever believeth in him should not perish, but have everlasting life" (John 3:16). God provided the way back to Him by His only Son, Jesus Christ, who became the spotless lamb that was "slain from the foundation of the world."

We are sinners; therefore we must repent of our sins. It is not the sins we have committed that makes us sinners, but we are sinners by Adam's choice in the garden. This is why we have all "sinned and come short of the glory of God."

"For by grace are ye saved through faith; and that not of yourselves: it is the gift of God" (Ephesians 2:8). We must repent of our sins (Acts 2:38; 3:19; 17:30). "That if thou shalt confess with thy mouth the Lord Jesus, and shalt believe in thy heart that God hath raised him from the dead, thou shalt be saved" (Romans 10:9). We must believe on Him and receive Him as our Savior. When we have repented of our sins we must be baptized and be careful we do not go back to our sins since we are a new creature (2 Corinthians 5:17). "He that hath my commandments, and keepeth them, he it is that loveth me: and he that loveth me shall be loved of my Father, and I will love him, and will manifest myself to him" (John 14:21). After you have become born again in Jesus Christ, enjoy your new life in Christ and be faithful and grow in Him (1 John 2:3; Romans 6:13; Revelation 2:10b).